celebrate

with me!

EDITED BY
Laura Gladwin

ILLUSTRATED BY
Dawn M. Cardona

MAGIC CAT PUBLISHING

CONTENTS

STAYING SAFE

The recipes and activities in this book are designed for children and adults to do together. Adult supervision is essential when using sharp knives, graters or scissors, cooking on the stove, or using mixers or blenders.

Before cooking, always wash your hands thoroughly. It's a good idea to wear an apron to protect your clothes and tie your hair back if it's long.

When cooking, an adult should be on hand to take things in and out of the oven, and to do any deep-fat frying. When deep-fat frying, wear long sleeves and stand well back. Do not fill the pan or fryer more than one-third full with oil, and never leave it unattended.

Hooray for the holidays!

Holidays and festivals are special days that bring joy and fun into our lives with feasting, dancing, special rituals and stories. They help us honour and remember the things that are important to us, connect with our families and communities, and mark out the stages of the year.

Each of us has different festivals we like to celebrate. Some of our festivities are the same, and some are unique to us.

In this book, twenty-five creative people from all around the world open their doors to share their favourite festival with us. Each person tells us why the festival is special to them and how they celebrate it, and shares the recipes and activities they do to celebrate, from cinnamon-dusted 'Carnival children' doughnuts, to Chinese dragon costumes, to felt Halloween pumpkins.

At the end of the book, you'll find tools to help you discover even more about festivals and some fun facts about how birthdays are celebrated too.

So, what are you waiting for?
Come celebrate with us!

NEW YEAR'S DAY

1 JANUARY

Hi, I'm Saeed Al-Rubeyi. I'm a fashion designer in Brighton. The first day of the new year is important in many cultures and has lots of traditions, like eating coin-shaped food to bring wealth or opening the windows to bring good luck.

People feel full of hope and new plans, and sometimes make New Year's resolutions for what they would like to do in the coming year.

I have a big meal with my family and go for a walk along the shore. Some years have happy memories and some have sad ones, but New Year's Day always brings a fresh start, and that's really exciting.

GO FOR A NEW YEAR'S NATURE WALK

Nature walks are fun at any time of year, but there's something extra special about getting outside on New Year's Day.

Being in nature – listening to the sounds, feeling the textures, smelling the fresh air – helps our brain, our mood and even our immune system, so what better way could there be to start the new year?

Why not create your own New Year's tradition by doing an activity on your walk? Perhaps you could talk about what your hopes are for the coming year, then collect one natural thing that you like – such as a pebble, a feather, a leaf, a twig or a pine cone – to represent each hope. When you get home, you could put them in a special jar to help you remember them. Or perhaps you could look out for one natural thing that you've never seen before to remind you that there's always something new to discover.

MAQLUBA

I'm half Iraqi, so I like to cook a traditional Iraqi dish called maqluba on New Year's Day. The name means 'upside down' because it's cooked in layers, then flipped upside down to serve. We're vegan, so we make our own version without meat. You can use any vegetables you like. Baharat is an Arabic spice blend that contains black pepper, coriander, cinnamon, cloves, allspice, cumin, cardamom and nutmeg.

SERVES 4
PREP TIME: 30 MINS
COOK TIME: 30 MINS

→ 1 onion
→ 1 large aubergine
→ 2 potatoes
→ 1 small head cauliflower
→ olive oil, for frying
→ 3 medium or
  2 large tomatoes
→ 250 g basmati rice
→ 2 teaspoons baharat
→ salt

Prepare the vegetables:

Slice the onion, aubergine and potatoes. Break the cauliflower into small florets. Heat some olive oil in a large frying pan over a medium heat. Fry each vegetable separately until lightly browned on each side. Remove and set aside.

Assemble the maqluba:

Grease a flameproof casserole dish or shallow pan with olive oil. Thickly slice the tomatoes, then cover the base of the pan with them. Add a layer of fried onions, then fried aubergine, then fried potatoes and fried cauliflower. Next, sprinkle in the rice and give the pan a little shake so the grains fall into the nooks and crannies. Then sprinkle over the baharat. Add 700 ml water and season generously with salt.

Cook the maqluba:

Cook over a medium-high heat until the water level drops below the top of the rice, then cover the pan and reduce the heat to low. Cook for 20–30 minutes, or until the rice is tender and a golden crust has started to form on the bottom. Leave it to stand for 10 minutes, then carefully turn it out onto a large serving plate. Don't worry if it's a mess – it always tastes amazing!

☼ LUNAR ☼
NEW YEAR

LATE JANUARY, EARLY FEBRUARY

Hello, my name is Lara Lee, and I'm a chef and food writer in London. My dad is Chinese-Indonesian and we always celebrate Lunar New Year (also known as Chinese New Year). It begins on the first new moon of the lunar calendar.

I love Lunar New Year because it's all about reuniting with family. Families get together for feasts and eat special foods like dumplings, which represent wealth. There are decorations, lanterns, firecrackers, dragon dances and parades in the streets. It's important to me to celebrate my heritage with my son and share these traditions with him.

SPICED SOY PORK LONGEVITY NOODLES

Popular during Lunar New Year, long noodles represent longevity (long life).

**SERVES 4-6
AS A MAIN COURSE
PREP TIME: 20 MINS
COOK TIME: 10 MINS**

→ 280 g dried egg noodles or 670 g fresh noodles (such as Hokkien)

→ 500 g skinless pork belly cubes

→ 2 tablespoons sunflower or rapeseed oil

→ 6 medium shallots, sliced

→ 2 red chillies, deseeded and sliced long (optional)

→ 6 tablespoons light soy sauce

→ 2 tablespoons brown sugar

→ 100 g kale, roughly chopped

→ 70 g roasted salted peanuts, plus extra to serve

→ 4 tablespoons oyster sauce

Cook the noodles:

In a large pan of boiling water, cook the noodles according to the package instructions. Drain and run them under cold water, then toss them in a little oil so they don't stick together.

Cook the pork:

Season the pork with salt. Heat the oil over a high heat in a large, deep, heavy-bottomed pan, add the pork and stir-fry for 4–5 minutes. Remove and set aside. Reduce the heat to medium, then add the shallots and chilis, if using. Cook for a few minutes until softened.

Finish the dish:

Increase the heat and return the pork to the pan with the soy sauce and sugar. Stir-fry for 2–3 minutes, or until the sauce is thick and sticky. Add the kale and cook for 1 minute, then add the cooked noodles, peanuts and oyster sauce. Stir until combined and heated through. Sprinkle with another handful of peanuts, then serve immediately.

MAKE A CHINESE DRAGON COSTUME

The dragon dance is a traditional Chinese dance performed during Lunar New Year. Many people operate one costume. It is believed that the longer your dragon, the more luck it brings!

Find a large cardboard box and cut a wide, smile-shaped hole through the front and into the two sides. Add cardboard teeth, ears and some curly strips below the mouth for a beard.

Cut out two small, round nostril holes above the mouth and attach two eyes to the top – painted paper coffee cups work well. If you like, you can paint the dragon head red. Red is a lucky colour.

Attach a long piece of red fabric for its body.

Put your dragon head on, grab some friends and get dancing!

VALENTINE'S DAY

14 FEBRUARY

My name is Tabara N'Diaye. My family is from Senegal, and now I run a basket-making business in the United Kingdom. My favourite festival is Valentine's Day. This special day has been celebrated since at least the fourteenth century.

Valentine's Day is a time to spread love. Traditionally, people send a card to someone to show that they care, and couples exchange gifts or share a special meal. I like to send handmade gifts to my friends and loved ones – little everyday tokens of my love that will make them smile when they see it.

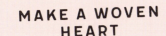

MAKE A WOVEN HEART

I often send handmade woven hearts on Valentine's Day. I love seeing how people use them — as a key ring or bookmark, in a purse or on their desk.

Cut 20 cm of basket-weaving reed or cane and soak it in lukewarm water for 5 minutes to soften it. Fold the two ends of the cane in to form a heart shape and secure it with a clothes peg. Glue the ends together and let dry for 24 hours.

Soak a small bundle of 20-cm canes for 5 minutes. Starting at the bottom right, weave a piece of cane under, then over, then under the frame of your heart. Leave the overhanging pieces.

Take another piece and start a row immediately above the previous one, doing the same thing but in reverse — threading it over, then under, then over. Continue in this way until your heart is completed. Using scissors, snip off all the excess cane.

Glue the ends of each row to the frame of the heart and let it dry.

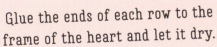

SHORTBREAD HEARTS

Taking inspiration from my woven hearts, my friend Philippa, who is an amazing baker, taught me how to make shortbread hearts to match. Give them as a gift or use them to decorate a cake.

MAKES ABOUT 12
PREP TIME: 1 HOUR
(INCLUDING CHILLING TIME)
COOK TIME: 8 MINS

→ 100 g plain flour
→ 50 g sugar
→ 100 g chilled butter, cubed
→ 200 g icing sugar
→ food colouring (optional)

Make the dough:

Sift the flour into a mixing bowl and stir in the 50 g sugar. Add the butter and rub it in with your fingertips until the mixture looks like breadcrumbs. Gently bring the dough together into a ball. Roll it into a log about 5 cm thick, wrap it tightly in cling film and chill in the fridge for 30 minutes to firm up.

Cut and bake the cookies:

Preheat the oven to 160°C. Use a sharp knife to slice thin circles of dough and shape them into hearts with your fingers. Bake for 8–10 minutes, or until lightly golden. Remove and leave to cool.

Make the icing:

Put the icing sugar in a bowl with a few drops of food colouring. Add a little water and stir to make a thick paste. If you'd like the icing to set firm, you can add a little powdered or fresh egg white. Pour it into a piping bag.

Decorate the cookies:

Once they have cooled, pipe a line of icing around the edge and down the middle of each one to match the frame of the woven hearts. Then pipe straight horizontal lines close together to make the biscuits look like woven hearts.

❧ CARNIVAL ❧

FEBRUARY OR MARCH

My name is Marta Veludo, and I'm a graphic designer. I'm originally from Lisbon, Portugal, but now I live in Amsterdam, Netherlands. I love to celebrate Carnival.

Carnival is a time of merriment, feasting, parties and parades. It's observed in many countries just before the Christian season of Lent, a solemn forty-day period of fasting and prayer.

When I was a child, I loved dressing up in costumes and playing pranks. It's a Portuguese tradition to bring a toy squeaky hammer to the Carnival parade to bop people on the head. My grandmother loved making fancy costumes for us to wear, and I always had at least three! I love this festival because you can be whoever you want to be.

MAKE A CARNIVAL MASK

It's fun to put together your own carnival costume. Why not finish it off with a homemade papier-mâché mask?

 Find a paper plate, or cut out a plate-sized circle of poster board.

 Make three equally spaced cuts from the edge halfway to the middle.

Overlap the cuts slightly and tape them together to make your mask 3D.

 Next, make a paste of flour and water in a bowl. Take strips of old paper or newspaper, dip them into the paste and stick them on the mask until it's covered with three or four layers. Create whatever shapes you like – maybe you'll add ears or a beard? Then let it dry completely.

When it's dry, cut out holes for your eyes and a small hole at each side for elastic string. Decorate with paint, feathers or stickers. Attach some elastic to the holes in the sides, and you're ready to go!

PORTUGUESE CARNIVAL DOUGHNUTS

Carnival dishes are often rich in fat, sugar and eggs because this is traditionally the last time people who observe Lent can eat them until Easter. These doughnuts are called filhoses de carnaval ('carnival children'), and they are absolutely delicious!

MAKES ABOUT 24
PREP TIME: ABOUT 1.5 HOURS
(INCLUDING RISING TIME)
COOK TIME: 10 MINS

- → 600 g plain flour
- → 1 packet (7 g) fast-acting instant yeast
- → 2 tablespoons sugar, plus extra for sprinkling
- → finely grated zest of 1 lemon
- → 50 g melted butter
- → 4 lightly beaten eggs
- → 100 ml lukewarm milk
- → vegetable oil, for frying
- → ground cinnamon, for sprinkling

Make the dough:

Sift the flour into a bowl and whisk in the yeast, sugar and lemon zest. Make a well in the middle and add the butter, eggs and milk. Stir to combine, gradually incorporating the flour until you have a soft dough. Tip it out onto a clean work surface and knead it until smooth. Cover and leave to rise until doubled in volume.

Fry the doughnuts:

Fill a deep-sided pan with 10 cm of vegetable oil. Set it over medium-high heat until it reaches 175°C (when a small piece of bread sizzles and turns brown in 20 seconds). Take a small piece of dough, flatten it a little and use your fingers to make a hole in the middle. Carefully place it in the hot oil and fry until deep golden brown, about 3 minutes on each side.

Serve:

Remove with a slotted spoon and drain on kitchen paper while you cook the rest. Sprinkle with sugar and cinnamon and serve immediately.

◈ INTERNATIONAL WOMEN'S DAY ◈

8 MARCH

Hello! My name is Juliet Sargeant, and I'm a garden designer in the United Kingdom. I enjoy celebrating International Women's Day. It's a global celebration of women's achievements that was started in 1911.

The celebration's theme is different each year, but the day is always about supporting women, recognizing their accomplishments and campaigning for true equality.

Although it doesn't shy away from some difficult issues, International Women's Day is inspiring and fills me with awe and hope. My daughters and I like to go for a walk and share a meal. We feel proud of what we have achieved, and think about ways we can support other women and girls.

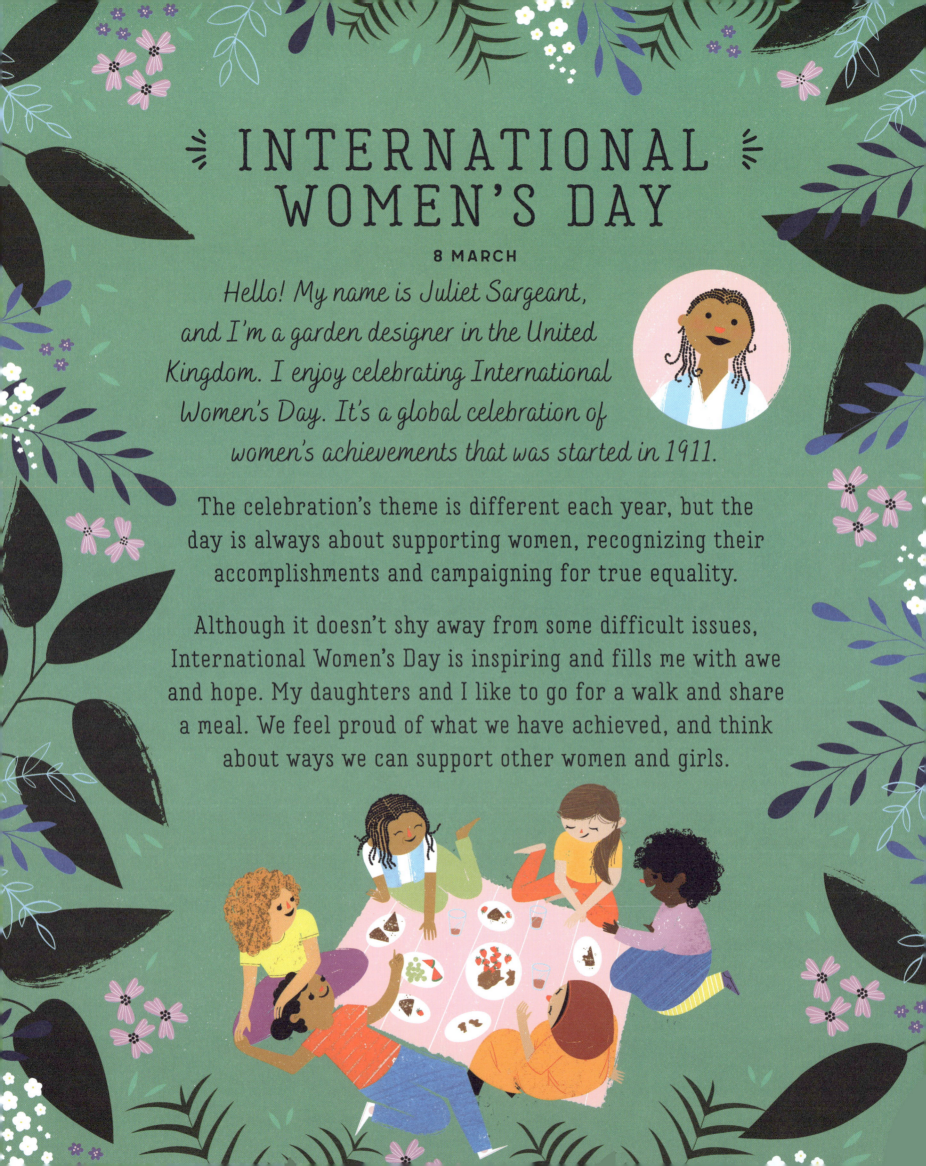

CARIBBEAN BANANA BREAD

This banana bread is a favourite from our old family recipe book, and I often bake it with my daughters for International Women's Day.

SERVES 6–8
PREP TIME: 15 MINS
COOK TIME: 50–60 MINS

→ 100 g soft margarine or butter
→ 175 g brown sugar
→ 4 large ripe bananas
→ 2 eggs, lightly beaten
→ 225 g plain flour, sifted
→ 1 teaspoon cinnamon
→ 1 teaspoon ground nutmeg
→ 1 teaspoon baking powder
→ ½ teaspoon bicarbonate of soda
→ ½ teaspoon vanilla extract

Prepare to bake:

Preheat the oven to 180°C. Grease a 900 g loaf tin and line it with baking paper. Put an ovenproof dish filled with water in the bottom of the oven.

Make the mixture:

In a mixing bowl, beat the margarine or butter with the brown sugar until creamy. Mash the bananas and stir them in. Beat the eggs into the mixture. Gradually stir in the flour, cinnamon, ground nutmeg, baking powder, bicarbonate of soda and vanilla extract. Stir well to make a smooth mixture.

Bake the banana bread:

Spoon the mixture into the loaf tin and bake for 50–60 minutes, or until firm but slightly springy to the touch. Remove from the oven and let it cool a bit before transferring to a cooling rack.

MAKE PAPER DOLLS

I like to support local campaigns that help women and raise awareness for women's equality. Perhaps there are some events happening near you that you could join?

Another nice way to celebrate is to make paper dolls. The way they hold hands shows how women have supported and celebrated each other over the years. You could decorate each one as a woman you admire – maybe that's your mum, your step-mum, your grandma or your teacher, or maybe it's a scientist like Jane Goodall, a poet like Amanda Gorman or an activist like Malala Yousafzai.

Take a long, rectangular strip of paper or card (around 12 x 30 cm).

Fold in half, then in half again, then in half again, to make a series of concertina folds.

With the folded edges on one side, draw half a female doll shape.

Cut it out carefully with scissors, then unfold and decorate your paper dolls.

HOLI

FEBRUARY OR MARCH

Hi, my name is Aishani Ghosh.
I'm a dancer specializing in
Bharatnatyam, a classical Indian dance.
My favourite holiday is Holi, the Hindu
festival of colour. It celebrates the triumph of good over evil
and the arrival of spring. It also marks the victory
of the god Vishnu over his foe, Hiranyakashipu.

Holi is all about laughter, happiness and celebration.
In India, people light special bonfires called holika and
go outside to sing, dance and throw gulal (brightly
coloured powder) or coloured water at each other,
revelling in the pure joy of colour.

At home in London, we visit the Hindu community centre or temple
and gather with family and friends for feasting and fireworks.

PAPRI CHAAT

In this popular street food from northern India, a crisp shell is filled with potatoes, chickpeas, yoghurt and chutney. It's a delicious, tangy taste explosion. Papri, sev and chaat masala are all available from South Asian food shops or online.

Cook the potatoes:

Cut the potatoes into small cubes and place in a pot of water. Boil until tender.

Make the chutney:

Place all the ingredients in a food processor and blend until fairly smooth.

Prepare the other ingredients:

In a bowl, combine the yoghurt and sugar. In another bowl, mix the sev with chilli powder, ground cumin, coriander and chaat masala.

Serve the papri chaat:

Arrange the papri on a large plate. Spoon some yoghurt onto each one, then top with potato, chickpeas and chopped onion. Drizzle with the chutney and tamarind chutney. Season with salt, sprinkle the sev mixture on top and serve immediately.

SERVES 6–8 AS A STARTER
PREP TIME: 30 MINS
COOK TIME: 10 MINS

→ 2 medium potatoes, peeled
→ 350 ml plain yoghurt
→ 2 teaspoons sugar
→ 100 g sev (fine crispy noodles)
→ ¼ teaspoon chilli powder
→ ¼ teaspoon ground cumin
→ 2 tablespoons chopped coriander
→ ½ teaspoon chaat masala (or use garam masala)
→ about 40 papri (crisp circular crackers)
→ 200 g canned chickpeas, drained
→ 1 onion, finely chopped
→ tamarind chutney, to taste
→ salt, to taste

For the chutney:

→ 2 large handfuls coriander leaves
→ 1 large handful mint leaves
→ 2–3 green chillies, roughly chopped (use less if you prefer)
→ 6 garlic cloves, roughly chopped
→ thumb-sized piece of fresh ginger, roughly chopped
→ 3 tablespoons lemon juice
→ ½ teaspoon cumin seeds
→ ¼ teaspoon asafoetida (optional)
→ pinch of salt

MAKE YOUR OWN GULAL

At Holi, we dress in white clothes, then go outside to throw gulal at each other. Why not try making your own colourful powders using natural ingredients?

To make red, grind dried hibiscus flowers to a powder. Alternatively, dry sliced or grated raw beetroot in the sun or in a low oven and grind it to a powder. You can also buy red sandalwood powder (rakta chandana).

To make yellow, mix ground turmeric with equal parts flour, such as gram (chickpea) flour, or try grinding dried marigold or calendula flowers.

To make green, dry out and grind green leaves, such as chard or spinach, or buy raw henna powder (mehndi) and combine it with gram (chickpea) flour.

To make blue, try drying and grinding jacaranda, blue hibiscus or any other blue flowers you can find.

For brown and black, grind tea leaves or ground coffee to a powder.

ST PATRICK'S DAY

17 MARCH

Hi, I'm Isobel Harbison, and I write and teach people about art. I live in London, but I grew up in Dublin, and my favourite Irish holiday is St Patrick's Day. It honours the patron saint of Ireland, who lived during Roman times, and it's a big celebration of all things Irish.

On St Patrick's Day, some people wear green, Ireland's national colour, and a shamrock, a three-leafed plant, which is the national symbol. Growing up, we used to watch the St Patrick's Day parade with its traditional Irish music and dancing. The River Liffey even used to be dyed green!

I love sharing the traditions with my children; it makes us feel connected with the country I come from and the millions of Irish people all around the world.

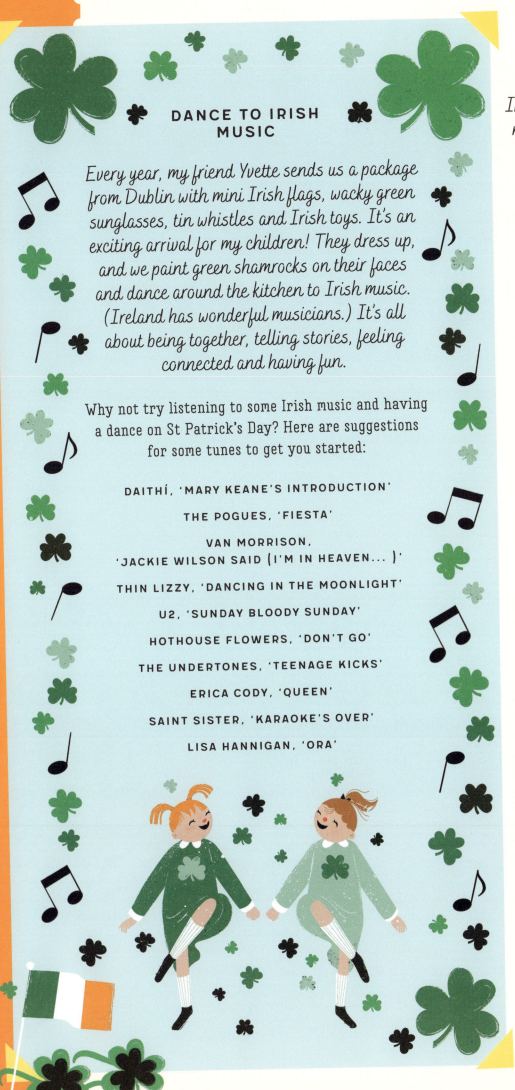

DANCE TO IRISH MUSIC

Every year, my friend Yvette sends us a package from Dublin with mini Irish flags, wacky green sunglasses, tin whistles and Irish toys. It's an exciting arrival for my children! They dress up, and we paint green shamrocks on their faces and dance around the kitchen to Irish music. (Ireland has wonderful musicians.) It's all about being together, telling stories, feeling connected and having fun.

Why not try listening to some Irish music and having a dance on St Patrick's Day? Here are suggestions for some tunes to get you started:

DAITHÍ, 'MARY KEANE'S INTRODUCTION'

THE POGUES, 'FIESTA'

VAN MORRISON, 'JACKIE WILSON SAID (I'M IN HEAVEN...)'

THIN LIZZY, 'DANCING IN THE MOONLIGHT'

U2, 'SUNDAY BLOODY SUNDAY'

HOTHOUSE FLOWERS, 'DON'T GO'

THE UNDERTONES, 'TEENAGE KICKS'

ERICA CODY, 'QUEEN'

SAINT SISTER, 'KARAOKE'S OVER'

LISA HANNIGAN, 'ORA'

MY MUM KATHLEEN'S IRISH SODA BREAD

Ireland is a lush, green island with lots of wonderful natural produce like root vegetables, meat and fish. To these we just add heat, salt and butter . . .

and a slice of traditional Irish soda bread.

MAKES 2 SMALL LOAVES
PREP TIME: 15 MINS
COOK TIME: 45 MINS

→ 50 g butter, cut into cubes, plus extra for greasing
→ 500 g wholemeal flour
→ handful of wheat bran
→ 2 tablespoons brown sugar
→ 1½ tablespoons bicarbonate of soda
→ pinch of salt
→ 1 egg, lightly beaten
→ 900 ml–1 litre buttermilk
→ 100 g sunflower seeds

Get ready:

Preheat the oven to 160°C and grease two loaf tins with butter.

Mix the dry ingredients:

Put the flour and wheat bran in a large mixing bowl. Add the butter and rub it into the flour with your fingers until the mixture looks like breadcrumbs. Stir in the sugar, bicarbonate of soda and salt.

Mix the dough and bake:

Stir in the egg and enough buttermilk to make a fairly wet mixture. Divide the mixture evenly between the loaf tins and sprinkle the tops with sunflower seeds. Bake in the oven for about 45 minutes, or until a skewer comes out clean.

EASTER

Hello! My name is Silvina de Vita. I'm an Argentinian designer and paper artist. The holiday I like best is Easter, or Pascua as we call it in Argentina. This is the Christian celebration of Jesus's miraculous return to life, called the Resurrection.

In Argentina, Pascua celebrations are all about family. When I was young, we went to church together every day during Semana Santa, or Holy Week, which is the week before Easter. On Good Friday, we'd watch the Via Crucis, a religious procession through the neighbourhood. On Easter Sunday, we always shared a big lunch together followed by a hunt for chocolate Easter eggs!

ROSCA DE PASCUA

This tasty Argentinian sweet bread is made in a ring shape to represent eternal life.

SERVES 6-8
PREP TIME: 3 HOURS
(INCLUDING RISING AND PROVING TIME)
COOK TIME: 40 MINS

→ 700 g plain flour
→ 14 g fast-action instant yeast
→ 100 g granulated sugar
→ 1 teaspoon salt
→ finely grated zest of 1 lemon
→ 4 lightly beaten eggs
→ 115 g butter, cubed and softened
→ 150 ml lukewarm milk
→ 1 tablespoon vanilla extract
→ glacé cherries, to decorate
→ pearl or demerara sugar, to decorate

For the pastry cream:
→ 300 ml milk
→ 2 teaspoons vanilla extract
→ 75 g sugar
→ 4 egg yolks
→ 2 tablespoons cornflour
→ 2 tablespoons plain flour

MAKE A 3D PAPER EASTER EGG

Eggs – a symbol of rebirth – have been associated with Easter for more than seven hundred years.

Draw or print out an egg template. Use it to cut out ten egg shapes using paper or card with different colours and patterns – whatever you like! Carefully fold all the eggs in half lengthways.

Glue one half of each folded egg to another half, and keep going, each time adding a new one, until you have used nine of the egg shapes. Before you glue the last one, add a loop of yarn or ribbon to the top so that you can hang it up.

Carefully open the sides and make sure they have even spacing between them, then leave to dry.

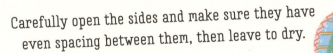

Make the dough:

Mix the flour in a large bowl with the instant yeast, sugar, salt and lemon zest. Add the eggs, butter, milk and vanilla extract. Gradually incorporate them into the flour and knead for about 5 minutes, or until smooth and elastic. Set aside, covered, until it has doubled in size.

Make the pastry cream:

Heat the milk and vanilla extract in a pan until almost simmering. In a separate bowl, whisk the sugar, egg yolks, cornflour and flour to make a paste. Gradually pour in the hot milk, whisking continuously. Return the mixture to the pan and cook over a low heat, stirring, until it simmers and thickens. Set aside to cool.

Shape the loaf:

Punch the dough down and shape it into a large circle. Make a big hole in the middle and put a ball of kitchen foil inside to hold its shape. Cover and leave to proof until almost doubled in size.

Bake and decorate the loaf:

Preheat the oven to 180°C. Bake the bread for 40 minutes, or until golden, then remove and leave to cool. Pipe the pastry cream in a ring around the top and decorate with glacé cherries and sugar.

❧ PASSOVER ❧
MARCH OR APRIL

My name is Lesléa Newman. I live and write in Massachusetts, USA. Passover, my favourite holiday, is the Jewish celebration of the Exodus of the Israelites from Egypt where they were once enslaved thousands of years ago.

During this holiday, we remember our ancestors, who had no time to wait for their bread to rise before they had to flee from Egypt. So, we do not eat anything made with yeast during Passover. Instead, we eat unleavened bread called matzo. We also share a festive meal called a Seder during which we eat special traditional foods. I include an orange on my Seder plate to represent people who are often excluded, such as the LGBTQ+ community, of which I am a member.

EXPLORE THE STORIES OF PASSOVER

At our Seder, we like to share stories that help us understand the ideas of Passover, such as what freedom means to us and how we can welcome all kinds of people into our lives.

Stories are a powerful way to connect with each other and talk about important things.

We also write down our favourite quotes about freedom on slips of paper and pass them around for guests to read aloud during Seder. For example, 'Freedom lies in being bold' (Robert Frost), or 'My liberty depends on you being free, too' (Barack Obama).

You could try something like that at home. Do you know any stories you could share with family and friends about welcoming strangers or being free? Perhaps you could all write down one sentence about what freedom means to you, then share your ideas around the dinner table.

THE BEST MATZO BREI IN THE WORLD

Matzo brei is delicious served with stewed apple, sugar and cinnamon, maple syrup or jam. You can find matzo in most large supermarkets or online.

SERVES 4
PREP TIME: 5 MINS
COOK TIME: 20 MINS

→ 7 large pieces of matzo
→ 3 eggs
→ 60 ml milk
→ pinch of salt
→ 2 tablespoons butter

Soak the matzo:

Break the matzo into small pieces in a large bowl and soak them in warm water for 1 minute, then drain. Beat together the eggs, milk and salt, then pour them onto the matzo and mix well.

Cook the first side:

Melt the butter in a large non-stick frying pan over low heat. Pour in the mixture, spreading it out evenly. Cook for about 10 minutes, until crisp and browned on the bottom.

Flip it:

Turn it over by placing a plate over the top of the pan and carefully flipping the pan over so the matzo brei falls onto the plate. Then slide the matzo brei back into the pan to cook the other side for another 10 minutes until brown and crisp. Cut into wedges and serve.

SONGKRAN

13 APRIL

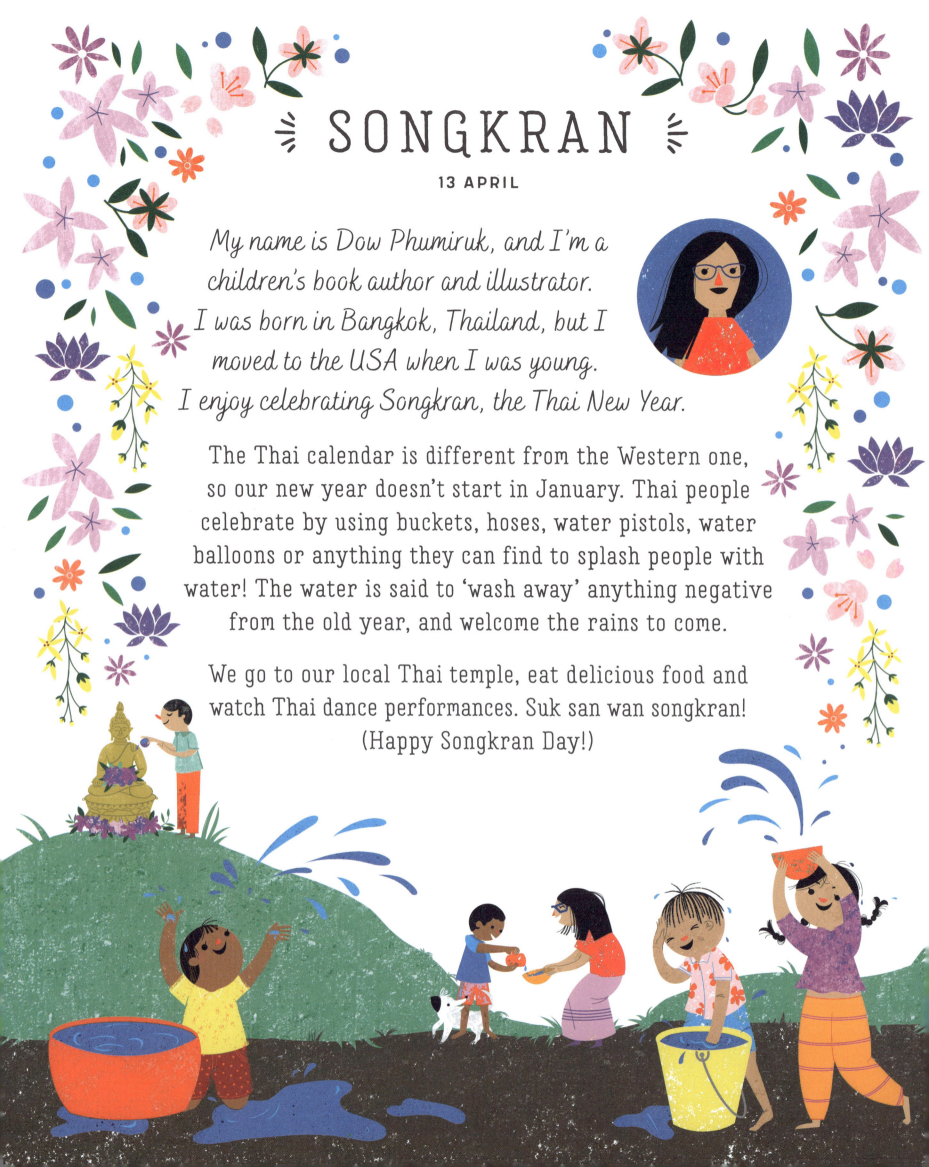

My name is Dow Phumiruk, and I'm a children's book author and illustrator. I was born in Bangkok, Thailand, but I moved to the USA when I was young. I enjoy celebrating Songkran, the Thai New Year.

The Thai calendar is different from the Western one, so our new year doesn't start in January. Thai people celebrate by using buckets, hoses, water pistols, water balloons or anything they can find to splash people with water! The water is said to 'wash away' anything negative from the old year, and welcome the rains to come.

We go to our local Thai temple, eat delicious food and watch Thai dance performances. Suk san wan songkran! (Happy Songkran Day!)

THAI-STYLE CONGEE

Congee is a kind of savoury, soupy porridge made from rice that is very popular in Asian countries. It is mostly eaten at breakfast, as well as late at night or as a comfort food when you are ill. Fish sauce is used a lot in Thai cooking. In recipes, it's delicious, but by itself it smells really icky, so don't sniff it or spill it!

SERVES 4–6
PREP TIME: 10 MINS
COOK TIME: 15 MINS

→ 2 tablespoons vegetable oil
→ 4 cloves garlic, finely chopped
→ 100 g chicken breast, sliced, or prawns
→ 500 ml chicken stock
→ 200 g cooked white rice
→ 2 tablespoons Thai fish sauce
→ 1–2 tablespoons rice vinegar, according to taste
→ 1 teaspoon salt
→ handful of chopped coriander, to serve
→ a handful of sliced spring onions, to serve

Cook the chicken or prawns:

Heat the oil in a pan over a medium-high heat. Add the garlic and stir-fry quickly; don't let it burn. Add the chicken or prawns and stir-fry until cooked through.

Add the rice and serve:

Add the chicken stock and bring to the boil, then add the cooked white rice, the Thai fish sauce, the vinegar and salt. Bring back to the boil and add the coriander and spring onions. Serve in bowls.

ASK YOUR ELDERS FOR BLESSINGS

There is a nice tradition in Thailand in which children can show respect to people who are older than them and ask for their blessing.

Collect some fragrant flower petals, such as jasmine, apple blossoms or roses, and put them in a large bowl of water.

Ask an older relative or friend to hold their hands as if in prayer over the bowl, while you use a smaller bowl to pour the fragrant water over their hands. Then, the older person should give you a blessing, such as wishing you good luck and good health in the coming year.

MOTHER'S DAY

FOURTH SUNDAY OF LENT

Hi, my name is Joanne Chang. I'm a pastry chef and restaurant owner from Massachusetts, USA. One of my favourite days is Mother's Day, because I love my incredible mum!

Mother's Day was started in 1907 by a woman named Anna Jarvis, who held a memorial service for her mother and wore a white carnation as a tribute. It gives us the chance to say thank you to the women who take care of us while we're growing up. My mum is my hero who has always supported me, and I love the chance to make her feel special.

MAKE A MOTHER'S DAY CARD

People love to give cards on Mother's Day, and there's nothing nicer than receiving a homemade one.

You could make your very own card with pictures of things your mother loves. Does she have a favourite flower, colour, type of food or animal? What activities does she enjoy? How could you include these in your design? Making your card unique and personal to her will make her feel extra special.

MAMA CHANG'S PORK AND CHIVE DUMPLINGS

When I was a kid, mum and I used to sit at the kitchen table, rolling and folding these dumplings together. We always eat her favourite dumplings in her honour on Mother's Day!

Serve with a dipping sauce of soy sauce with black vinegar and sliced ginger.

MAKES ABOUT 40
PREP TIME: 30 MINS
COOK TIME: 15 MINS

→ 8 leaves Chinese (Napa) cabbage
→ 1 tablespoon salt
→ 450 g ground pork
→ 50 g minced chives or garlic chives
→ 3 tablespoons light soy sauce
→ 1 tablespoon finely chopped ginger
→ 2 teaspoons toasted sesame oil
→ 1 pack ready-made circular dumpling wrappers
→ 2 tablespoons vegetable oil

Prepare the filling:

Thinly slice the cabbage, toss it in a bowl with the salt, then set aside for 10 minutes. Put the pork, chives, soy sauce, ginger and sesame oil in another bowl and mix well with your hands. Squeeze as much liquid as you can out of the cabbage, then mix it into the pork.

Make the dumplings:

Place a dumpling wrapper on a clean work surface. Add one tablespoon pork filling, then dip your finger in water and moisten the edge of the wrapper. Fold it over into a half-moon shape and press together at the top. Pinch and fold along the edge to make a pleat and seal the dumpling (you can find tutorials online). Continue with the rest of the wrappers and filling.

Cook the dumplings:

Heat the vegetable oil in a large non-stick frying pan with a lid. Add a single layer of dumplings and cook over medium heat for about 3 minutes, without moving them, until the bottoms are a deep golden brown. Add two tablespoons water and put the lid on tightly. Cook for 2 minutes, shaking the pan occasionally. Add another two tablespoons water. Repeat this process twice. Finally, remove the lid and increase the heat to evaporate any water and crisp up the bottoms. Serve immediately.

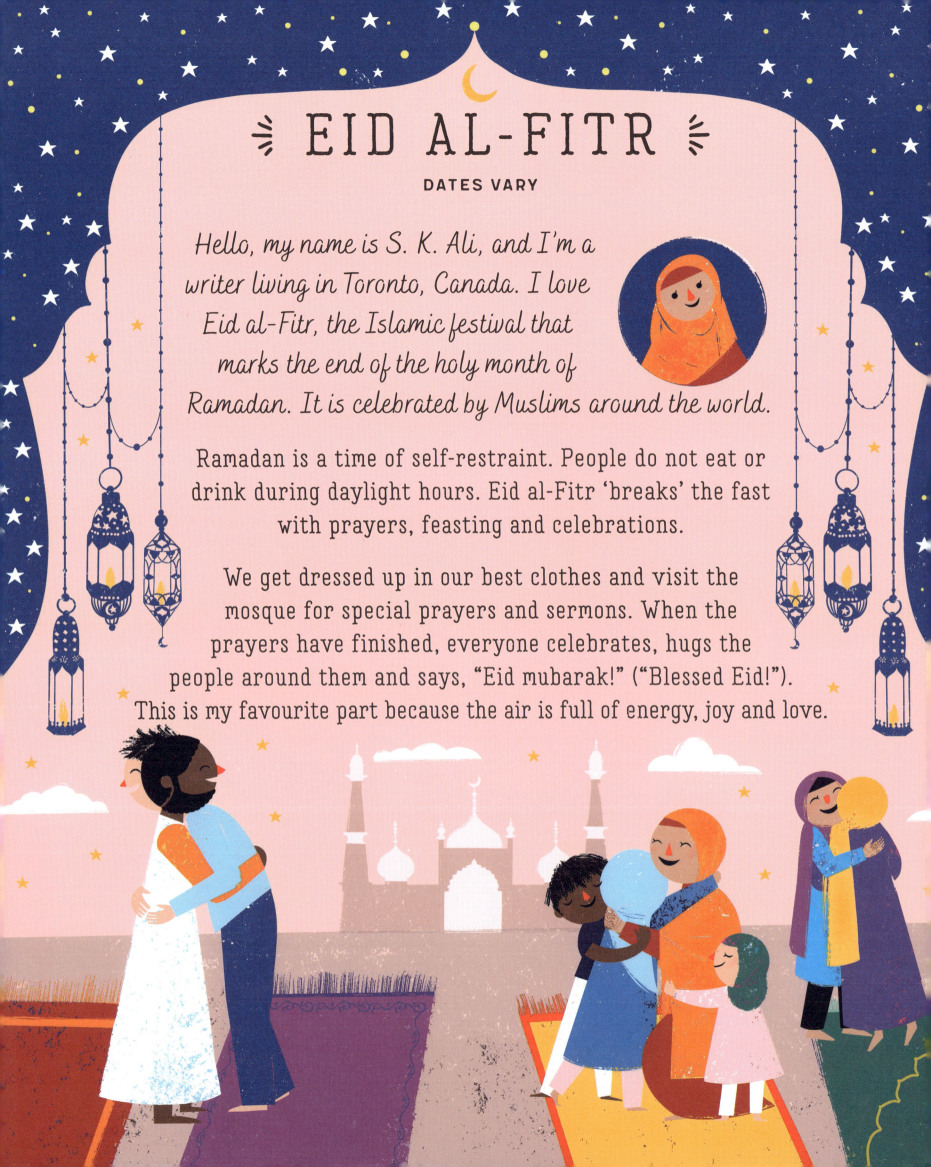

⇒ EID AL-FITR ⇐

DATES VARY

Hello, my name is S. K. Ali, and I'm a writer living in Toronto, Canada. I love Eid al-Fitr, the Islamic festival that marks the end of the holy month of Ramadan. It is celebrated by Muslims around the world.

Ramadan is a time of self-restraint. People do not eat or drink during daylight hours. Eid al-Fitr 'breaks' the fast with prayers, feasting and celebrations.

We get dressed up in our best clothes and visit the mosque for special prayers and sermons. When the prayers have finished, everyone celebrates, hugs the people around them and says, "Eid mubarak!" ("Blessed Eid!"). This is my favourite part because the air is full of energy, joy and love.

MAKE HENNA HAND PRINTS

Part of the fun of Eid is preparing for the celebrations and deciding what you're going to wear.

In some Muslim cultures, we have a party the night before when friends and family gather to decorate our hands with henna, or mehndi as it's called in India and Pakistan. It's so much fun to be together and feel excited about Eid!

You could make a decoration by drawing carefully around your hand on a piece of paper to make an outline, then decorating it with lots of swirly lines and shapes. Try a design using flowers, leaves, moons or stars. Or look online for traditional henna designs.

SHAKEELA'S PINEAPPLE PUDDING

This easy dessert is absolutely delicious and has become an essential part of my family's Eid al-Fitr celebrations. The recipe originally came from my Saudi cousin, Shakeela. Kashta (sometimes called kaymak) is a type of very rich, thick cream used in the Middle East.

SERVES 6
PREP TIME: 2–3 HOURS
(INCLUDING SETTING TIME)

→ 85 g halal pineapple jelly cubes or crystals
→ 1 x 170 g tin kashta or double cream
→ 1 x 397 g can sweetened condensed milk
→ 400 g chopped fresh pineapple or tinned crushed pineapple, drained
→ 20 g flaked almonds, toasted

Make the jelly:

Prepare the pineapple jelly according to the instructions on the box and put it in the fridge to set.

Purée:

Once set, put the jelly into a food processor along with the kashta (or double cream) and condensed milk. Blend into a smooth purée.

Assemble the dish:

Cover the bottom of a rectangular dish with the pineapple. Pour the puréed cream and jelly mixture over the top, making sure the liquid is level. Sprinkle the almonds on top and put in the fridge to set for at least half an hour before serving.

JUNETEENTH

19 JUNE

Hi, I'm Michael Platt. I'm a baker and food justice advocate – and an American school kid! One of my favourite holidays is Juneteenth. It commemorates 19 June 1865, the day when the news that slavery had been outlawed finally reached the last enslaved people in Galveston, Texas.

People celebrate Juneteenth with church services, community gatherings and parades. In our family, we come together to remember, tell stories and make food that reminds us of our heritage – like jollof rice, barbecues and red velvet cakes.

Over the generations, Black voices have often been represented negatively, but Juneteenth is a chance to celebrate our important African American culture, which is a great, empowering feeling.

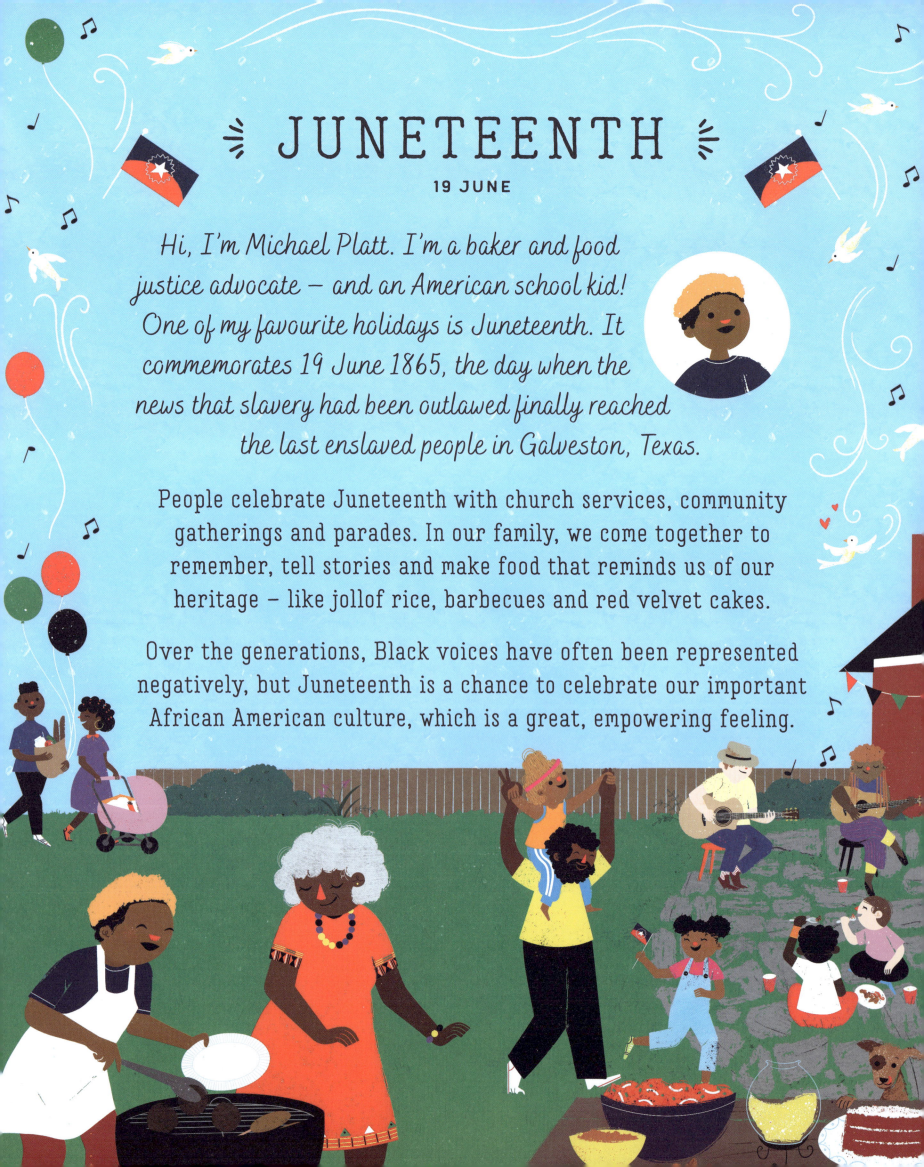

WATERMELON AND TOMATO SALAD

Tomatoes and watermelon are tastiest in summer, and their bright red colour is perfect for Juneteenth, as the colour red represents freedom and strength. To pick a good watermelon, knock on it to see if it sounds hollow, which means it's juicy. If there is a pale yellow spot, it means it wasn't picked too early, which is good.

SERVES 8
PREP TIME: 10 MINS

→ 1 ripe watermelon, cut into 5-cm cubes
→ about 8 vine-ripened tomatoes, cut into 2-cm pieces
→ 1 red onion, thinly sliced
→ 120 ml virgin olive oil
→ 4 tablespoons red wine vinegar
→ 1 teaspoon sugar, plus extra to taste
→ cayenne pepper, to taste
→ ½ teaspoon salt, plus extra to taste
→ black pepper to taste
→ handful of chervil or parsley, chopped

Make the dressing:

Put the watermelon, tomatoes and onion in a large bowl. In a medium bowl, whisk together the oil, vinegar, sugar, cayenne, salt, pepper and chervil or parsley. Taste the dressing and adjust it to your liking. Some people like it tangy and add more vinegar. If you have a really sweet watermelon, you may want to reduce the sugar.

Finish the salad:

When you're happy with the dressing, pour it over the watermelon, tomatoes and onions. Toss well, cover and let it sit in the fridge for about 20 minutes. Toss again before serving and, using a slotted spoon, transfer to another bowl (this gets rid of the excess juice). Serve cold with more dressing on the side, if you like.

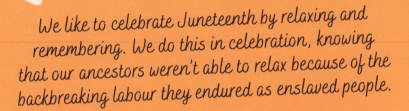

CELEBRATE BLACK CULTURE

We like to celebrate Juneteenth by relaxing and remembering. We do this in celebration, knowing that our ancestors weren't able to relax because of the backbreaking labour they endured as enslaved people.

Why not celebrate Black culture by listening to music, checking out art or reading books by Black artists and writers?

You could also show your support by making your own Juneteenth flag and displaying it in your window. The flag was created in 1997, and each part of it has a special meaning. The star represents the state of Texas and the enslaved people freed in all states. The starburst outline represents a new beginning. The curved line is the horizon, showing the promising future that lies ahead. The red, white and blue remind us that enslaved people, and their descendants, were and are Americans. The date 19 June 1865, is the original Juneteenth.

To make your flag, draw these shapes on rectangular paper and attach to a wooden craft stick with tape or glue.

SUMMER SOLSTICE

NORTHERN HEMISPHERE: 21 OR 22 JUNE
SOUTHERN HEMISPHERE: 21 OR 22 DECEMBER

Hello, I'm Miquita Oliver, and I'm a television broadcaster in London. My favourite festival is the summer solstice. This is the longest day of the year, when the sun sets late in the evening.

Although they don't fall on the same day, Midsummer's Day and the summer solstice are celebrated in similar ways, traditionally with a bonfire. When I was growing up, we often visited my aunt in Sweden for the midsummer festival. People wear flower crowns, dance around a pole covered in flowers and celebrate nature and the sun.

These days, we have a party outdoors, eating and drinking as the sun sets and feeling connected to the earth, sun and moon.

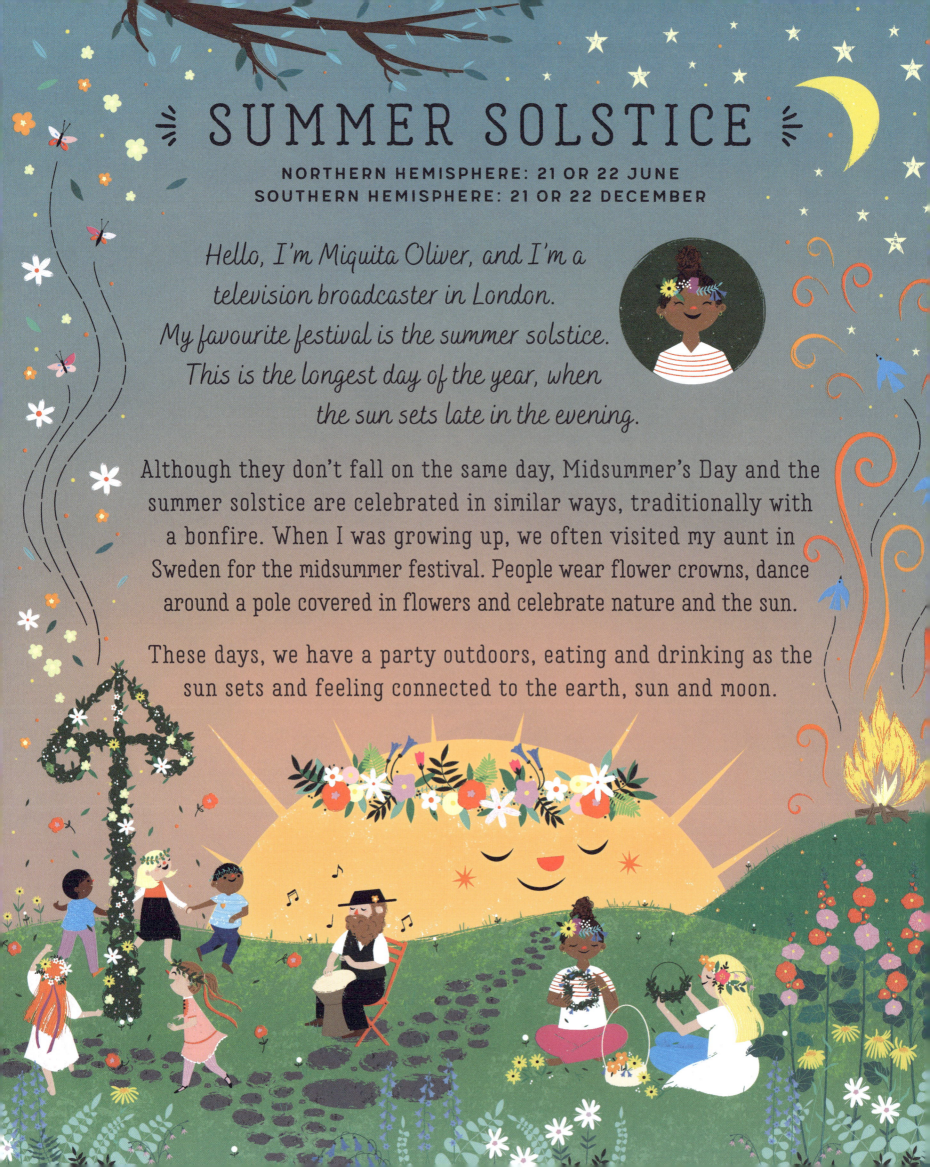

HEALING CHICKEN SOUP

My Swedish cousin Naima has a beautiful garden full of herbs and plants growing so high you could almost get lost in them. She serves this wonderful soup at our solstice party.

SERVES 8
PREP TIME: 30 MINS
COOK TIME: 1¾ HOURS

→ 2 onions, peeled and quartered
→ 1 free-range chicken
→ 8 black peppercorns
→ 2 carrots (for the stock)
→ 1 large tomato, quartered
→ chunk of fresh ginger
→ 1 cinnamon stick
→ half head of garlic
→ 1 celery stick
→ 1 chilli (optional)
→ 2 beetroots, peeled and chopped
→ 2 carrots (for the soup), peeled and chopped
→ 250 g chestnut mushrooms, sliced
→ 1 chopped leek
→ large handful of chopped greens, such as kale or spinach
→ handful of chopped fresh herbs, such as dill, parsley, mint or thyme

Make the soup base:

Put the onions into a large cooking pot with the chicken, peppercorns, carrots, tomato, ginger, cinnamon stick, garlic, celery and chilli, if using. Cover with water and add a large pinch of salt. Bring to a boil and simmer for 1¼ hours, or until the chicken is tender, skimming it occasionally.

Add the vegetables:

Strain the liquid into another large pan. Set the chicken aside. Add the beetroot, carrots, mushrooms and leek to the liquid. Simmer for 15 minutes, then add the greens and simmer for 10 minutes more.

Finish the soup:

Meanwhile, take the chicken meat off the carcass and cut it into small chunks. Shortly before serving, put the chicken in the pan along with the fresh herbs. Season with salt and pepper and serve with more herbs on the side.

CREATE NATURE ART

People celebrate the summer solstice in all kinds of ways. In northern Europe, it has been marked since ancient times with stone circles, bonfires, dancing and feasting until the sun comes up. Magic was thought to be at its strongest at this time, thanks to the power of the sun.

At our solstice celebrations, we light a fire and write down our intentions or hopes on pieces of paper and throw them into the fire. As the sparks fly up, it feels as though the world is listening.

What special ritual could you create to mark the summer solstice? Think about what you would like the rest of the year to bring and write down your thoughts on pieces of paper. Then create some nature art by arranging leaves, twigs and stones into a circle or in any way you like, and place your intentions underneath, as a special way to remember them.

≈ FATHER'S DAY ≈

THIRD SUNDAY IN JUNE

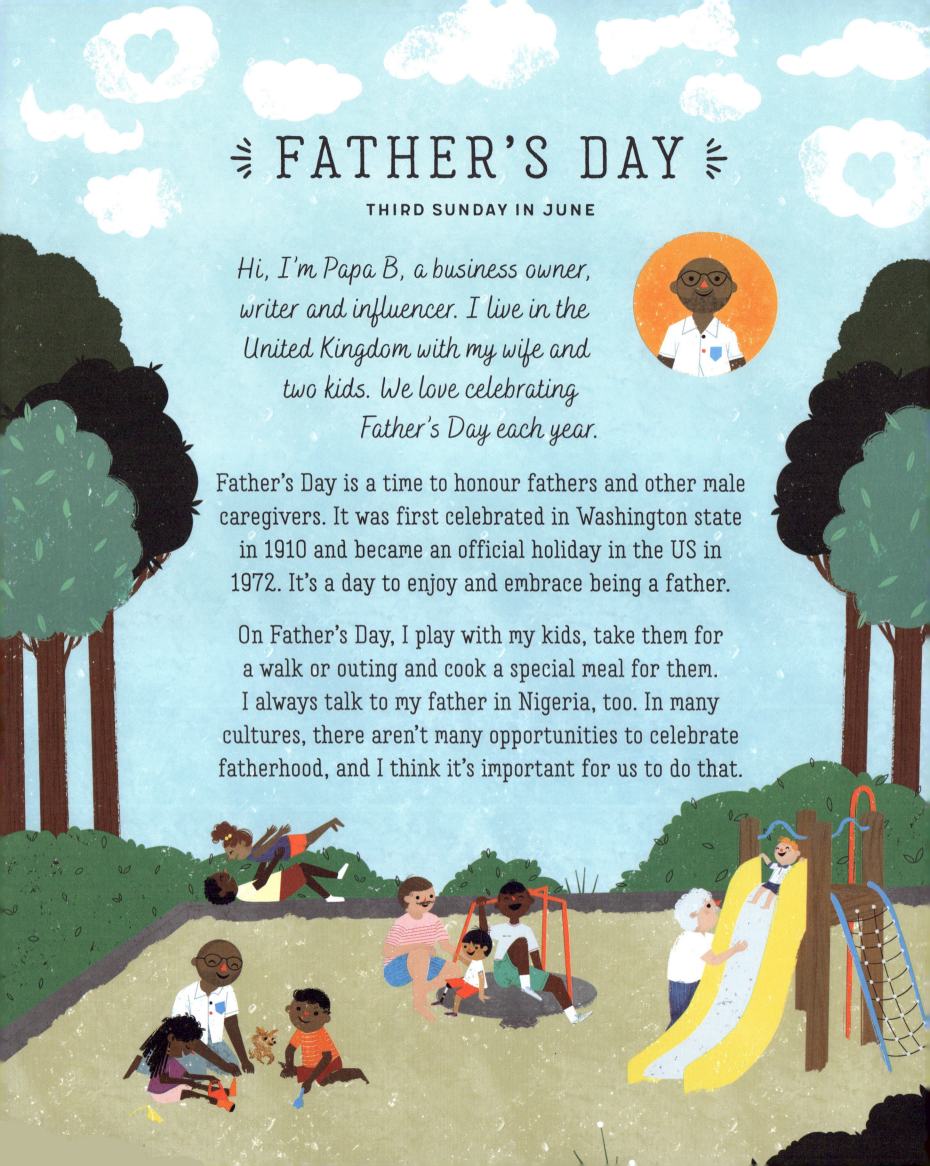

Hi, I'm Papa B, a business owner, writer and influencer. I live in the United Kingdom with my wife and two kids. We love celebrating Father's Day each year.

Father's Day is a time to honour fathers and other male caregivers. It was first celebrated in Washington state in 1910 and became an official holiday in the US in 1972. It's a day to enjoy and embrace being a father.

On Father's Day, I play with my kids, take them for a walk or outing and cook a special meal for them. I always talk to my father in Nigeria, too. In many cultures, there aren't many opportunities to celebrate fatherhood, and I think it's important for us to do that.

PLAY A GAME OF WHO KNOWS DAD

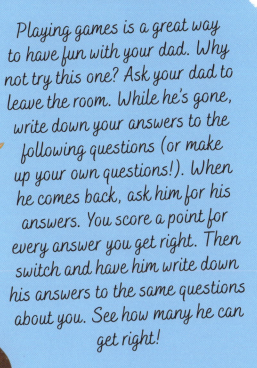

Playing games is a great way to have fun with your dad. Why not try this one? Ask your dad to leave the room. While he's gone, write down your answers to the following questions (or make up your own questions!). When he comes back, ask him for his answers. You score a point for every answer you get right. Then switch and have him write down his answers to the same questions about you. See how many he can get right!

→ What's your favourite colour?

→ What's your least favourite household chore?

→ Which animal would you most like to be?

→ What's your favourite sport?

→ Which would you rather give up: pasta, cheese or chocolate?

→ Which superhero power would you choose: an invisibility cloak, the ability to fly or eyes that shoot laser beams that can cut through anything?

→ How tall are you?

→ Where would you most like to go on holiday?

PAPA B'S MINCED BEEF

I love cooking for my family. My speciality is this tasty minced beef, which can be served in so many ways: with rice or pasta, on a baked potato or wrapped in a tortilla. You can vary the ingredients to suit your taste. I like to serve it with quartered hard-boiled eggs and buttered long-grain white rice on the side.

SERVES 6-8
PREP TIME: 20 MINS
COOK TIME: 40 MINS

→ 1 tablespoon olive oil
→ 1 onion, finely chopped
→ 3 bell peppers, chopped
→ 100 g shiitake mushrooms, sliced
→ 1 Scotch bonnet chilli, chopped (optional)
→ 450 g minced beef (I use 15 per cent fat)
→ 1 teaspoon Caribbean all-purpose seasoning
→ ¼ teaspoon flavour enhancer (optional)
→ 1 chicken or beef stock cube
→ handful of fresh spinach leaves
→ 200 g raw jumbo prawns, peeled

Cook the vegetables:

Heat the oil in a large pan and add the onion, peppers, mushrooms and chilli, if using. Cook for 5 minutes, until softened.

Add the meat:

Use a fork to break up the beef. Add this to the pan and cook, stirring, to brown the meat. Add the seasoning, flavour enhancer and crumble in the stock cube. Cook for 30 minutes, stirring occasionally and adding a splash of water if needed.

Finish the dish:

Finally, add the spinach and prawns and simmer for 5 minutes, or until the prawns are cooked through.

MID-AUTUMN FESTIVAL

Hello, my name is Queenie Chan and I'm a manga artist. I live in Sydney, Australia, but I'm originally from Hong Kong. My favourite holiday is the Mid-Autumn Festival — or Zhongqiu Jie in Mandarin. It's a celebration of the harvest moon and an important holiday in East Asian communities around the world.

During the festival, families gather to eat, light lanterns, pray for good fortune and gaze at the moon, which is bright, big and full at this time of year. People make offerings to Chang'e, the Chinese moon goddess, and her companion, the Jade Rabbit. I love being with my family and seeing the moon in all its glory.

MOON CAKES

~~~

MAKES 10-12 SMALL CAKES
PREP TIME: 1¼ HOURS
(INCLUDING RESTING TIME)
COOK TIME: 25 MINS

Moon cakes are an essential part of the Mid-Autumn Festival. They are beautifully decorated, palm-sized pastries filled with a sweet bean or lotus paste and the yolk of a salted duck egg in the middle. People usually buy moon cakes, but you can make your own. Salted duck eggs and sweet lotus or red bean paste can be found online or at Asian supermarkets. You can get creative with your own decorations, or use a moon cake mould.

→ 75 g honey
→ 2 tablespoons vegetable oil
→ 125 g plain flour, plus extra for dusting
→ pinch bicarbonate of soda
→ salted duck egg yolks (optional)
→ 300 g sweet lotus or red bean paste
→ 1 egg, lightly beaten

Make the pastry:

In a bowl, mix the honey and oil. Sift in the flour and bicarbonate of soda and mix them together to form a soft dough. Knead it gently for a minute. Cover with cling film and set aside for at least 30 minutes.

Prepare the filling:

Pat the salted egg yolks dry with kitchen towel (if using). On a clean, lightly-floured surface, take a golf ball–sized piece of red bean or lotus paste and flatten it into a circle. Place an egg yolk on top, then carefully wrap the paste around it, pinching and rolling with your fingers to create a sphere. Repeat with the remaining filling.

Finish the cakes:

Preheat the oven to 180°C. Take a golf ball–sized piece of pastry and roll it out into a thin circle. Place a filling ball on top and carefully shape the pastry around it to enclose it, pinching it closed. Roll it gently to even out the pastry layer. Dust with flour and place in a moon cake mould, or press down gently to create a flat top and decorate with a skewer or cookie stamp. Repeat with the remaining pastry. Chill in the fridge for 15 minutes. Brush the cakes very lightly with the beaten egg and bake for 20–25 minutes, or until golden brown. Cool before serving.

MAKE A RABBIT LANTERN

Lanterns are lit during the Mid-Autumn Festival and create a beautiful, festive atmosphere. They come in all kinds of shapes and designs.

Begin with five paper plates and four doilies. Take four paper plates and cut out the circles in the centre, leaving just the rims. Glue paper doilies onto the rims of the four plates. Decorate the centre of one of the doilies to look like a rabbit face. Make two ears and glue them on top. Staple the rabbit face and the other three doily plates together to make a square shape.

Staple an uncut paper plate to the bottom to make the base. If you want to hang your lantern, attach four equal pieces of string to the four sides and tie them together at the top. Add a flameless tea light or mini LED light and your lantern is ready!

DIWALI

OCTOBER OR NOVEMBER

My name is Sonali Shah, and I'm a television broadcaster in London. I love Diwali, the festival of lights, which is celebrated by millions of Hindus, Sikhs and Jains around the world. It marks new beginnings and the triumph of good over evil, light over darkness.

Diwali is celebrated in different ways, but usually involves lighting small oil lamps called divas or diyas and creating beautiful patterns called rangolis. People also pray, visit the temple, feast with family and watch fireworks.

When I was young, I loved dressing up in special clothes for the celebrations. Now I enjoy sharing the traditions with my children, visiting friends and family and eating delicious Indian food.

DIWALI BHEL

I love Indian street food, and this version of classic bhel puri is fantastic — so fresh and vibrant! The ingredients and quantities are up to you, but be sure to include tangy chutney and crunchy sev mamra (available from South Asian food shops or online). If I'm taking it somewhere, I put everything in a bowl except the sev mamra which I add just before serving so it doesn't lose its crunch.

Prepare the fillings:

Cook the potatoes in a pot of boiling water until tender, then drain and cool. Cook the quinoa according to package instructions. Prepare the other fillings you wish to use and put each filling in a separate bowl.

Make the green chutney:

Roughly chop the coriander leaves and stalks. Place all the ingredients in a small food processor with 1 tablespoon water. Blend to a coarse purée, adding more water if needed.

Assemble the components:

Put the green chutney, tamarind chutney, sev mamra, yoghurt, chaat masala, pomegranate seeds, if using, chopped nuts and coriander in separate small bowls. Arrange them next to the bowls of prepared fillings.

Serve your Diwali bhel:

Tell your guests to prepare their own bhel just how they like it by layering the ingredients on a small plate, finishing with yoghurt, coriander, pomegranate seeds, chaat masala, nuts and sev mamra. Eat right away.

SERVES 6-8
PREP TIME: 30 MINS
COOK TIME: 15 MINS

Your choice of the following fillings:
→ 2 potatoes, peeled and cubed
→ 200 g quinoa
→ 400 g canned chickpeas or mung beans, drained
→ 1 onion, finely chopped
→ 200 g cherry tomatoes, halved

For the green chutney:
→ 30 g coriander, plus extra leaves to serve as a component
→ 2 cloves garlic, peeled
→ 1 green chilli, deseeded (optional)
→ freshly squeezed juice of 1 lime

For the components:
→ 100 g tamarind chutney
→ 200 g sev mamra (crispy puffed rice and noodles; you can use crushed crisps instead)
→ 500 g plain yoghurt
→ 1 tablespoon chaat masala or garam masala
→ 1 tablespoon pomegranate seeds (optional)
→ 200 g cashews or peanuts, roughly chopped

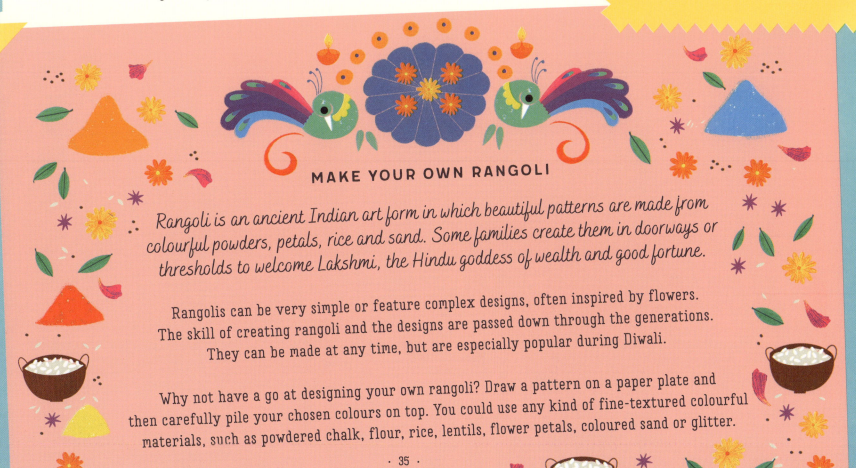

MAKE YOUR OWN RANGOLI

Rangoli is an ancient Indian art form in which beautiful patterns are made from colourful powders, petals, rice and sand. Some families create them in doorways or thresholds to welcome Lakshmi, the Hindu goddess of wealth and good fortune.

Rangolis can be very simple or feature complex designs, often inspired by flowers. The skill of creating rangoli and the designs are passed down through the generations. They can be made at any time, but are especially popular during Diwali.

Why not have a go at designing your own rangoli? Draw a pattern on a paper plate and then carefully pile your chosen colours on top. You could use any kind of fine-textured colourful materials, such as powdered chalk, flour, rice, lentils, flower petals, coloured sand or glitter.

HALLOWEEN

31 OCTOBER

My name is Mike Aspinall, and I'm a craft blogger. My favourite festival is Halloween — the festival of spooky things. The name comes from All Hallows' Eve, the night before the Christian celebration of All Saints' Day.

Halloween traditions are also drawn from Samhain, an ancient Celtic festival at the beginning of winter when the spirits of dead people were thought to visit. People lit bonfires and wore costumes to scare away evil spirits.

I love to fill my house with skeletons, ghosts, bats and witches. Children wear costumes and go trick-or-treating, and people enjoy carving pumpkins and placing a candle inside them to make them glow.

WELCOME

MAKE PUMPKIN DECORATIONS

Sewing is one of my favourite hobbies. During the Halloween season, I like to sew small pumpkin decorations from felt, which I give as gifts or hang around my house.

Cut out two identical round pumpkin shapes from orange felt, and one from black felt. Draw shapes for the eyes and mouth on one of the orange pieces, then cut them out carefully.

Layer the three shapes together with the black in the middle, then sew all the way around the edge with embroidery thread or waxed cotton. Finally, tie off the loose ends of the thread and add a small loop of thread to hang it with. You can add a small piece of black felt for the stem, if you like. You can also make these decorations in the shapes of ghosts or bats – whatever you like!

ROASTED PUMPKIN SEEDS

It's traditional to carve pumpkins for Halloween — but what happens to all the seeds? I like to roast them in a tasty spice mix for a seasonal snack. You can vary the spices as you wish.

SERVES 6 AS A SNACK
PREP TIME: 5 MINS
COOK TIME: 10 MINS

→ seeds from 1 large pumpkin
→ 4 teaspoons olive oil
→ 3 teaspoons mixed spices (I use smoked paprika, garlic powder, cumin and salt)

Prepare the seeds:

Preheat the oven to 180°C and line a baking sheet or tray with baking paper. Rinse the seeds in running water to remove the pumpkin flesh, then spread them out on a clean towel and pat them dry.

Spice them up:

In a bowl, mix the olive oil with the spices. Add the dried pumpkin seeds to the bowl and toss them until the seeds are coated.

Roast and serve:

Spread the seeds on the baking tray and roast them for around 10 minutes. Let them cool, then enjoy as a snack or sprinkle them over salads or soup.

DAY OF THE DEAD

1–2 NOVEMBER

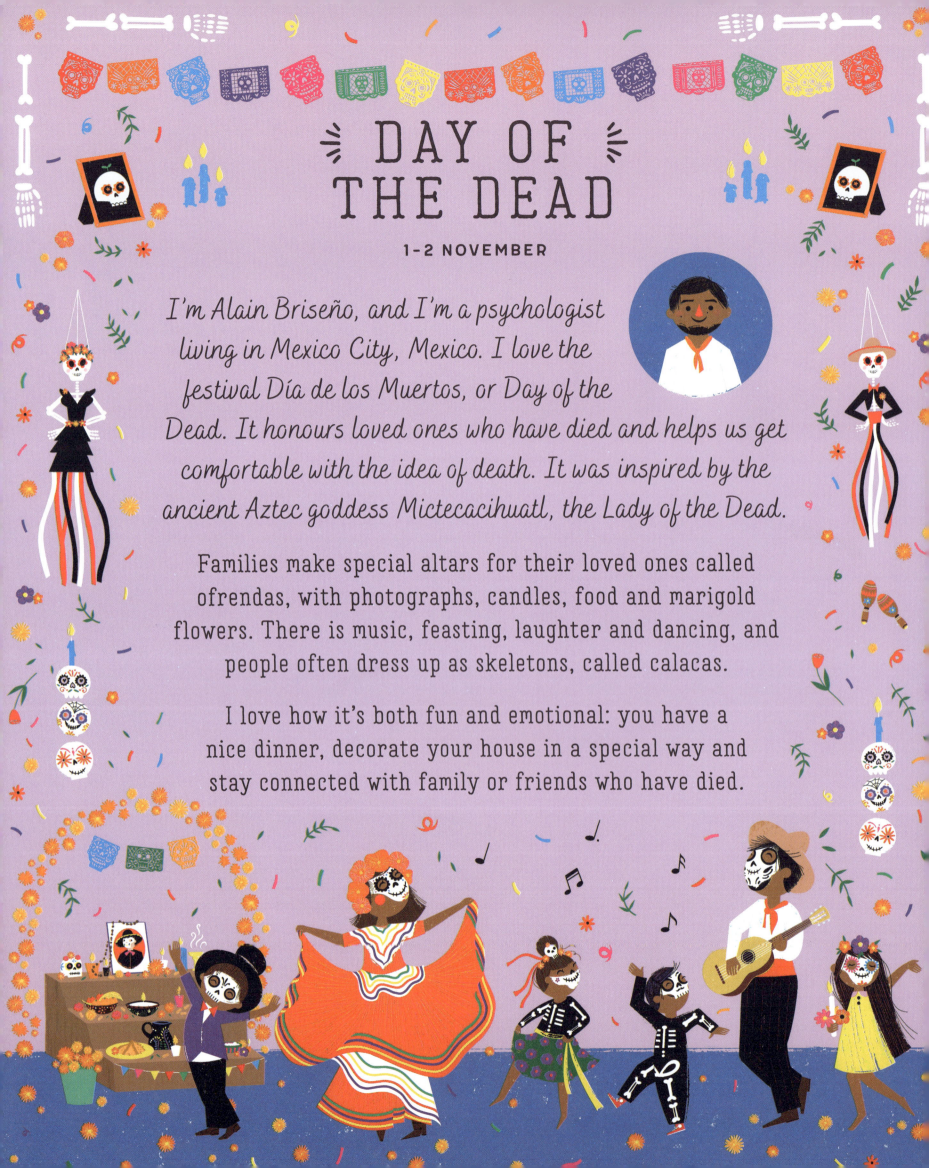

I'm Alain Briseño, and I'm a psychologist living in Mexico City, Mexico. I love the festival Día de los Muertos, or Day of the Dead. It honours loved ones who have died and helps us get comfortable with the idea of death. It was inspired by the ancient Aztec goddess Mictecacihuatl, the Lady of the Dead.

Families make special altars for their loved ones called ofrendas, with photographs, candles, food and marigold flowers. There is music, feasting, laughter and dancing, and people often dress up as skeletons, called calacas.

I love how it's both fun and emotional: you have a nice dinner, decorate your house in a special way and stay connected with family or friends who have died.

MAKE YOUR OWN ALTAR

Why not make an altar to honour someone who has died, and who you want to remember? It could be a family member, a pet or a person who has inspired you.

First, find a place to build it: a clear, flat surface, such as a shelf or small table. Cover the surface with orange flowers or petals – ideally marigolds, but you could use any orange or yellow flowers, or make them out of paper.

Arrange some of the following items on top: photographs of the person, small candles, a glass of water or some of the foods or drinks that the person enjoyed. Traditionally, you also add some coffee and salt.

Make some paper cut-out skeleton decorations (look up calacas online), maybe some little skulls too, and arrange these on the altar.

Have a special dinner with your family, then light the candles and share your best memories of the person.

MEXICAN HOT CHOCOLATE

The most traditional Day of the Dead dish is pan de muertos (bread of the dead), a sweet bread with a cross on top, but most people buy it ready-made. I have it with this delicious Mexican hot chocolate. Feel free to add your own ideas to the recipe!

SERVES 1
PREP TIME: 5 MINS
COOK TIME: 5 MINS

→ 90 g good-quality chocolate, ideally with a high cocoa percentage
→ 200 ml milk
→ 1 tablespoon double cream
→ pinch of cinnamon

Melt the chocolate:

Cut the chocolate into small chunks. Heat half the milk in a small pan over a medium heat until it starts to steam. Reduce the heat to low, add the chocolate pieces, and whisk until they have melted completely.

Finish it off:

Add the rest of the milk and the double cream and stir until the mixture is hot, but don't let it boil again. Carefully pour it into a mug, add a pinch of cinnamon on top and it's good to go!

BONFIRE NIGHT

5 NOVEMBER

Hello, I'm Nick Wood, and I'm an architect and artist from London. I enjoy celebrating Bonfire Night. It's a British festival that marks the day in 1605 when a group of unlawful people led by Guy Fawkes tried to blow up the Houses of Parliament in London by hiding barrels of gunpowder in the cellar. Thankfully, they didn't succeed!

Today, Bonfire Night – also called Guy Fawkes Day – is celebrated across the United Kingdom with bonfires and fireworks.

I like to host a big bonfire party, and friends and family join us for an evening of food, fire and fireworks.

MARSHMALLOW SPARKLERS

SERVES AS MANY AS YOU LIKE
PREP TIME: 10 MINS

→ 90 g good-quality chocolate
→ 1 packet marshmallows
→ hundreds and thousands

We love toasting marshmallows until they are gooey in the middle and toasted on the outside. Watch out, though, as they get super hot! Here's another fun marshmallow treat to share on Bonfire Night... no toasting required.

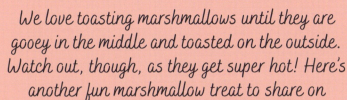

Melt the chocolate:

Break the chocolate into small pieces and place it in a microwave-safe bowl. Microwave on medium-high until the chocolate melts, stirring every 15 seconds. (Alternatively, place the chocolate in a heatproof bowl set over a pan of barely simmering water and stir until melted.)

Prepare the marshmallows:

Place one marshmallow onto the tip of a wooden skewer. Repeat with as many skewers as you have. Put the sprinkles out into a small bowl.

Dip and go:

Dip each marshmallow into the melted chocolate so that just the top is coated, then dip them into the hundreds and thousands. Set the skewers upright for 30 minutes, or until the chocolate has set.

BUILD A BONFIRE

On Bonfire Night, I like to escape London to my parents' house in the countryside. My dad, brother and I spend the day building a bonfire.

With help from an adult, you could try building your own fire in a fireplace or fire pit.

If you don't have a safe place to make a real fire, why not create a fire craft? At this time of year, there are often lots of brightly coloured autumn leaves around. If you don't have leaves available, you can make some out of tissue paper or sugar paper.

Gather or cut out some different coloured leaves and some twigs too. Glue your twigs horizontally onto a piece of cardboard, overlapping them slightly. Arrange your leaves on top like flames and stick them down with glue. Put the yellow ones at the bottom, the orange ones next and finally the red ones at the top.

HANUKKAH

LATE NOVEMBER, DECEMBER

My name is Erin Gleeson, and I write and paint pictures for cookbooks. I live in the California mountains with my family, and every year we observe Hanukkah.

It's the Jewish festival of miracles and bringing light into dark places. We have a special candelabra called a menorah that has eight branches, one for each day of Hanukkah, and we add a new candle each night.

We eat fried potato pancakes called latkes and jelly doughnuts called sufganiyot at our Hanukkah party. Traditionally, children are given gifts of money or chocolate coins called gelt. We also donate money, called tzedakah, to help people who need more light in their lives.

MAKE YOUR OWN MENORAH

It's easy to make your own menorah — you just need eight candle holders in a row and one in the middle, which is called the shamash (this means 'helper'). You use the shamash to light the eight main candles.

You can make a lovely menorah with citrus fruits. For this, you'll need four limes, one orange and nine thin candles. Cut the limes in half, and cut the bottom off the orange. Make little holes in the rounded top of each lime half and in the rounded top of the orange. Line the lime halves up with the orange in the middle and insert a candle into the orange. Each night during Hanukkah, use the orange candle to light another candle and insert it into one of the limes until all eight are lit.

COURGETTE LATKES

Food fried in oil is traditional at Hanukkah because it represents the miracle of a tiny amount of oil that kept burning for eight days in the Temple of Jerusalem, and potato latkes are one of the most popular Hanukkah dishes. We often add courgette or sweet potato to our latkes. They're often served with apple sauce, but I like them topped with Greek yoghurt, chopped chives and pomegranate seeds.

MAKES ABOUT 24
PREP TIME: 20 MINS
COOK TIME: 15 MINS

→ 2 medium potatoes (about 300 g)
→ 2 medium or 1 large courgette (about 270 g)
→ 50 g fresh breadcrumbs
→ 3 eggs, lightly beaten
→ pinch of garlic powder
→ salt and pepper
→ olive oil, for frying

Grate the vegetables:

Peel and grate the potatoes, then grate the courgette and mix together. Scoop the mix into a clean cloth and squeeze out any liquid.

Make the latke mixture:

Transfer the grated vegetables into a bowl and mix in the breadcrumbs, eggs and garlic powder. Season with salt and pepper.

Fry the latkes:

Heat some olive oil in a large frying pan over a medium heat. Place heaped tablespoons of the latke mixture into the pan and fry until golden brown on both sides, turning over carefully. Serve immediately.

WINTER SOLSTICE

NORTHERN HEMISPHERE: 21 OR 22 DECEMBER
SOUTHERN HEMISPHERE: 21 OR 22 JUNE

*Hello, my name is Shikira Alleyne-Samuel,
and I'm a textile designer in London.
My favourite festival is the winter solstice. It's
the shortest day of the year, with the fewest hours of daylight.*

We celebrate the solstice in our own special way,
drawing on different traditions, such as Yule, an ancient
pagan midwinter festival. We are also inspired by
Kwanzaa and the ancient Egyptian celebration of the
return of the sun god, Ra, at the winter solstice.

Our festivities help us appreciate life, love, nature
and our roots. We gather to decorate a Tree of Life
and have family dinners to celebrate the warmth of the
sun, since daylight increases after the winter solstice. We
also honour themes from Kwanzaa, such as cooperation,
creativity and working together.

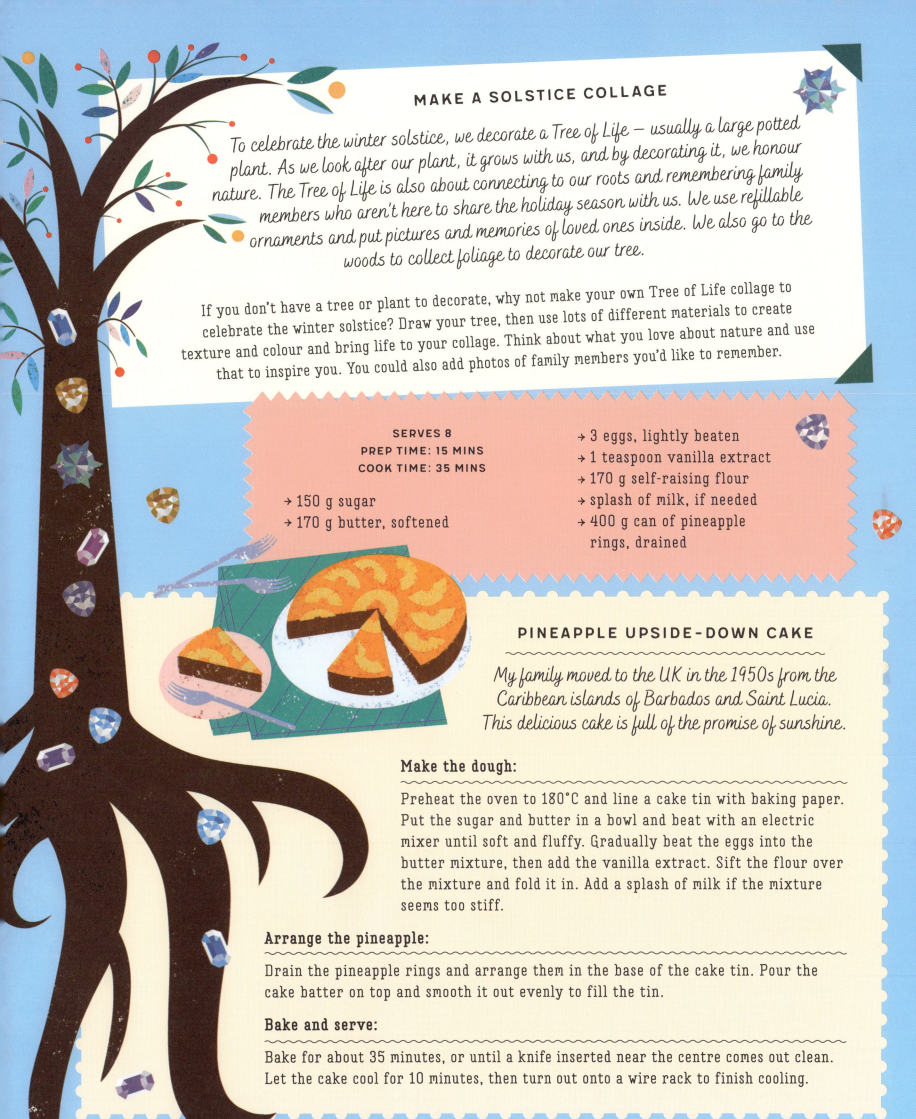

MAKE A SOLSTICE COLLAGE

To celebrate the winter solstice, we decorate a Tree of Life — usually a large potted plant. As we look after our plant, it grows with us, and by decorating it, we honour nature. The Tree of Life is also about connecting to our roots and remembering family members who aren't here to share the holiday season with us. We use refillable ornaments and put pictures and memories of loved ones inside. We also go to the woods to collect foliage to decorate our tree.

If you don't have a tree or plant to decorate, why not make your own Tree of Life collage to celebrate the winter solstice? Draw your tree, then use lots of different materials to create texture and colour and bring life to your collage. Think about what you love about nature and use that to inspire you. You could also add photos of family members you'd like to remember.

SERVES 8
PREP TIME: 15 MINS
COOK TIME: 35 MINS

→ 150 g sugar
→ 170 g butter, softened

→ 3 eggs, lightly beaten
→ 1 teaspoon vanilla extract
→ 170 g self-raising flour
→ splash of milk, if needed
→ 400 g can of pineapple rings, drained

PINEAPPLE UPSIDE-DOWN CAKE

My family moved to the UK in the 1950s from the Caribbean islands of Barbados and Saint Lucia. This delicious cake is full of the promise of sunshine.

Make the dough:

Preheat the oven to 180°C and line a cake tin with baking paper. Put the sugar and butter in a bowl and beat with an electric mixer until soft and fluffy. Gradually beat the eggs into the butter mixture, then add the vanilla extract. Sift the flour over the mixture and fold it in. Add a splash of milk if the mixture seems too stiff.

Arrange the pineapple:

Drain the pineapple rings and arrange them in the base of the cake tin. Pour the cake batter on top and smooth it out evenly to fill the tin.

Bake and serve:

Bake for about 35 minutes, or until a knife inserted near the centre comes out clean. Let the cake cool for 10 minutes, then turn out onto a wire rack to finish cooling.

CHRISTMAS

25 DECEMBER

Hello! I'm Marta Sanchez, a jazz pianist and composer living in New York City, USA. I'm originally from Spain and my favourite holiday is Christmas, or Navidad as we call it in Spanish. Christmas is the day Christians celebrate the birth of Jesus.

In Spain, we celebrate on Christmas Eve and usually eat roast lamb or suckling pig. I love spending time with my whole extended family and eating a lot of food! We sing and play Christmas carols, exchange gifts, go to church and nibble Spanish cookies and sweets that you only find at this time of year. Continuing these traditions every year makes Christmas very special.

CELEBRATE WITH SONG

Christmas is a very special time of year in Spain, filled with music and song as well as good things to eat. The traditional festive songs are called *villancicos*, and they are similar to the Christmas carols in other countries. For my family, singing together is our favourite part of the celebrations. Songs are a great way to learn a bit of Spanish too!

Why not put on a concert of festive songs for your family this year? You could include your favourite carols and try out some new ones. You could even swap in some Spanish phrases for English ones. Singing is a fun way to learn some Spanish!

'Jingle Bells' is 'Cascabeles' (pronounced cas-car-bell-es).

'We Wish You a Merry Christmas and a Happy New Year' is 'Feliz Navidad a Todos y Año Nuevo También' (pronounced fe-lees nav-i-da a-toe-dos ee an-yo nwe-vo tam-byen).

TURRÓN DE NAVIDAD

This chewy, nutty sweet was invented more than five hundred years ago. It's very popular in Spain at Christmas.

MAKES ABOUT 50 SMALL PIECES
PREP TIME: 2-3 HOURS
(INCLUDING SETTING TIME)
COOK TIME: 20 MINS

→ 180 g whole blanched almonds
→ 500 g honey
→ 2 sheets edible wafer paper
→ 4 egg whites

Toast the almonds:

Preheat the oven to 190°C. Spread out the almonds on a baking tray and roast for 10 minutes, or until golden and toasty.

Heat the honey:

Pour the honey into a large pan and bring to a boil over a medium heat. Remove from the heat and set aside. Line a roasting tin or shallow oven dish with edible wafer paper.

Whisk the egg whites:

Put the egg whites in a large, clean bowl and whisk with an electric mixer until stiff peaks form. Carefully and slowly pour the honey onto the egg whites, whisking continuously, then return the mixture to the pan.

Cook the mixture:

Cook over a medium heat for 15–20 minutes, stirring gently. It should increase in volume at first, then turn a dark golden colour. Pour a spoonful onto a plate and put it in the fridge. If it sets firm after a minute, it's ready.

Leave to set:

Stir the almonds into the mixture and quickly pour it into the lined dish. Place another sheet of wafer paper on top and cool in the fridge for 2–3 hours. Cut into small pieces to serve.

KWANZAA

26 DECEMBER–1 JANUARY

Hello! My name is Nadia Hohn, and I'm an author, writer and teacher from Toronto, Canada.

My favourite celebration is Kwanzaa, which celebrates African family and social values. It was created in 1966 by Dr Maulana Karenga, an American professor of Africana studies. Each day of Kwanzaa is dedicated to one of the seven values (Nguzo Saba): unity (umoja), self-determination (kujichagulia), collective responsibility (ujima), cooperative economics (ujamaa), purpose (nia), creativity (kuumba) and faith (imani). Each value has its own symbol. There's also a community feast on the final day, called the karamu.

I celebrate by meditating on the seven values. I love how Kwanzaa makes me feel centred and so proud of my African origins. It helps me feel connected to other Black people around the world, regardless of their religion or belief system.

JAMAICAN PUMPKIN SOUP

SERVES 6
PREP TIME: 20 MINS
COOK TIME: 1 HOUR

People often eat traditional African dishes during Kwanzaa. For me, it's the Jamaican pumpkin soup we ate every Saturday when I was growing up. It's usually made with beef, but this one is vegetarian. If you can't find Caribbean cock soup mix online or in the supermarket, substitute three tablespoons tapioca starch or cornflour with two teaspoons turmeric and one teaspoon each of thyme, celery seed, black pepper, smoked paprika and onion granules.

Make the soup base:

Bring the vegetable stock to the boil in a large pan and add half the pumpkin. Simmer for 10 minutes, then lift out the pumpkin, purée it, and return it to the liquid to form the base of your soup.

Add the vegetables:

Add the rest of the ingredients except the coconut milk, parsley and onion granules and simmer for 30 minutes. Add the remaining ingredients and simmer for 15–20 minutes more, or until all the vegetables are tender and the soup has thickened.

Season and serve:

Taste and add salt if needed. Remove the chilli, allspice berries and thyme stems before serving. If you prefer a thicker texture, purée a little more of the pumpkin.

(Recipe adapted from thatgirlcookshealthy.com)

- → 2 litres vegetable stock
- → 450 g pumpkin, chopped (traditionally this is calabaza, a green-skinned pumpkin, but any squash will work)
- → 1 x 400g can jackfruit, drained and shredded
- → 1 cho cho (christophine or chayote) or courgette, chopped
- → 2 carrots, chopped
- → 1 sweet potato, chopped
- → 250 g yam, preferably yellow yam, chopped (or you could use swede or turnip)
- → 3 tablespoons cock soup mix
- → 3 spring onions, chopped
- → 4 garlic cloves, chopped
- → 6 sprigs thyme
- → 1 Scotch bonnet chilli
- → 10 pimento (allspice) berries
- → 250 ml coconut milk
- → ½ tablespoon chopped parsley
- → 1 teaspoon onion granules
- → salt, to taste

MAKE A MKEKA

*I often make a paper mkeka (decorative table mat) with my students for Kwanzaa.
To make one, you need two large equal-sized squares of paper in different colours, scissors and glue.*

Fold the first piece of paper in half and use scissors to make straight cuts from the fold up to about 2.5 cm from the top. The cuts should be about 2.5 cm apart. Open it out and you should have a square with long slots and an uncut border.

Take the second piece of paper and cut it into 2.5 cm strips. Cut additional paper if you would like more colours.

Taking one strip at a time, weave it over and under the slots in the first piece, pushing them up towards the top and securing each end with glue. Alternate the weave on each strip and secure with glue as you go.

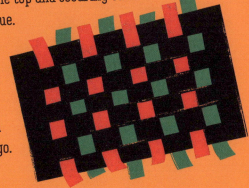

You can use your mkeka as a place mat, or to display the symbols of the seven values of Kwanzaa, such as the communal cup, candle holder, maize, fruit and vegetables and gifts.

NEW YEAR'S EVE

31 DECEMBER

My name is Wendy Shearer, and I'm a writer and storyteller in the United Kingdom. My favourite festival is New Year's Eve. The last day of the year is celebrated all around the world with parties, feasting and fireworks.

I enjoy bringing the year to a close with stories and family gatherings. In our family, we all share our favourite thing that happened that year. Then we say something we're hopeful for in the new year. We count down to midnight, watch London's Big Ben chime twelve times on TV, make a champagne toast and wish one another a Happy New Year.

I love that it's a festival everyone can take part in and celebrate in their own way with warmth and cheer.

STONE SOUP

I like to tell this traditional story on New Year's Eve. Everyone joins in by adding an ingredient. Sometimes we get creative and add a hope for the new year to the soup to make the story more magical.

A long time ago, and just as far away, a stranger was travelling across the highlands of Guyana. He wandered into a village on New Year's Eve, where the villagers were eating fried chickpeas.

"Please may I have some food?" he asked hungrily. But the villagers refused, saying they barely had enough for themselves.

"If you let me have a pot and some water, I can make stone soup," the stranger said.

"Stone soup?" they cried. The villagers were intrigued and watched as he put a stone in a pot of boiling water over their fire. He stirred it, then took a sip.

"How is it?" they asked. "It needs a little salt," said the stranger. Someone passed him some salt. He stirred again, before taking a sip.

"How is it?" they asked. "Maybe some carrots would help the flavour," he replied. A villager gave him a carrot. He put it in, stirred and stirred, then took a sip.

"A piece of beef would be good," the stranger said, and someone passed him a beef bone. He added it, stirred the soup, and took a sip. "Hmmm, perhaps an onion," he said.

This continued until the pot was brimming with ingredients. "What is the magic behind this stone?" asked one villager, eager to try the soup. "There is no magic in the stone," the stranger replied, "only a sprinkle of joy and hope from everyone who has contributed to the pot."

COOK-UP RICE

My parents are from Guyana in South America, and I always make a traditional Guyanese dish of 'cook-up' rice at New Year. It's a humble, heartwarming dish that reminds us that no matter what challenges we face, we always have abundance, even if it's a simple pot of rice. You can add other things (traditionally pig's tail and chilli peppers!), but this is the way I like it.

SERVES 8
PREP TIME: 20 MINS
COOK TIME: 30 MINS

→ 1 tablespoon oil
→ 1.3 kg chicken pieces on the bone (thighs, legs or wings), cut into chunks
→ salt, to taste
→ freshly ground black pepper, to taste
→ 1 onion, finely chopped
→ 2 garlic cloves, finely chopped
→ 300 g canned chickpeas, drained
→ 1 x 400 g can coconut milk
→ 350 g long-grain rice
→ small bunch of fresh thyme
→ 4 spring onions, chopped
→ 3 bay leaves

Fry the chicken:

Heat the oil in a pan. Season the chicken pieces with salt and pepper. Add them to the pan, skin side down. Fry until the skin has browned, then remove the chicken and add the onion, garlic and black pepper to the pan. Fry for a few minutes until softened. Add the chickpeas and stir for 2 minutes.

Add the rice:

Next, add 470 ml water, the coconut milk, rice, thyme, spring onions and bay leaves. Bring to a boil, then return the chicken to the pan and season with salt and pepper. Stir well, cover the pan and simmer for 30 minutes, or until the liquid has been absorbed. Serve hot.

BIRTHDAYS AROUND THE WORLD

In this book, we have looked at different kinds of celebrations from around the world. But what about the one many of us look forward to the most: our birthday?

You might think that all birthdays involve parties, presents, birthday cake, blowing out candles and singing 'Happy Birthday'. But people around the world have different birthday traditions. In parts of the Middle East, some people don't celebrate their birthday at all. In Vietnam, everyone celebrates their birthday on New Year's Day, which is called Tét. People gather to feast with their families, exchange gifts and watch fireworks, parades and dragon dances.

Finding out how people celebrate is a great way to learn about different cultures and countries. Families often have their own traditions too.

Here are some birthday traditions that you might not know about...

HAVING FUN

In **Jamaica**, it's traditional to throw flour (and sometimes eggs too!) at the birthday boy or girl. This is called flouring.

In **Canada**, people often have butter rubbed on their nose when it's their birthday. This is supposed to stop bad luck from sticking to them.

A fun **Mexican** birthday tradition, which has become popular elsewhere, is the piñata. This is a shape, usually an animal, made out of papier-mâché, with sweets inside. Partygoers hit the piñata with sticks until the sweets fall out.

'Giving the bumps' is an **Irish** birthday tradition: the special person is lifted by their arms and legs by two or more adults and bumped (carefully) on the floor, once for each year of their life.

In **Denmark**, a flag is flown outside the house when it's someone's birthday. As in many other European countries, it's traditional for the birthday person to bring a cake to share with friends and colleagues, rather than having one made for them.

EATING

Noodles are traditionally eaten on people's birthdays in **China** because they represent longevity (having a long life).

In **Russia**, on your birthday you are often given a pie with your name on it!

In **South Korea** you eat seaweed soup, called miyeok guk, for breakfast on your birthday.

Special birthday sweet treats include:

→ brigadeiros (chocolate truffles) in **Brazil**

→ fairy bread (white bread rolled up with butter and rainbow sprinkles) in **Australia**

→ sweet mochi rice cakes in **Japan**

→ taarties (little fruit pies) in the **Netherlands**

SPECIAL BIRTHDAYS

In some cultures, certain birthdays have extra importance. In **Jewish** tradition, girls and boys celebrate their bat mitzvah or bar mitzvah when they turn twelve or thirteen with special religious ceremonies.

In **Nigeria**, your 1st, 5th, 10th and 15th birthdays are the most significant. They are celebrated with big parties with lots of guests and traditional foods like jollof rice and roasted goat.

In some parts of **Latin America**, when a girl turns fifteen, she has a quinceañera celebration, when she wears a special dress and has a big party with family and friends.

YOUR BIRTHDAY

How do you celebrate your birthday?

Do you do any of the things mentioned here?

Does your family have its own special birthday traditions?

If you could invent a new way to celebrate your birthday, what would it be?

MORE FUN WITH FESTIVALS

There are so many festivals celebrated around the world.
In this book, we have looked at just a few of them.

Festivals are wonderful for bringing people together with their families and communities. They celebrate all kinds of things that are important to people, like religious beliefs, events in history, the changing seasons or the values that people hold dear. Some are held on fixed dates, and some vary each year.

These special days often involve feasting on special foods; putting up colourful, joyful decorations; praying, singing, dancing and telling stories; exchanging gifts or cards; visiting special places like temples, mosques or churches; and doing things you can't do on any other day! They also mark the passage of time and help bring rhythm to the year.

By discovering which holidays people enjoy, and how they celebrate them, we can connect with different cultures and learn what's important to them.

Why not ask the people around you which festivals they like to celebrate? Here are some ideas for questions you could ask. You can add your own too!

WHAT IS YOUR FAVOURITE FESTIVAL?

WHAT IS IMPORTANT ABOUT IT?

WHY IS IT SPECIAL TO YOU?

WHAT DOES YOUR FAMILY DO TO CELEBRATE?

WHAT ARE THE TRADITIONAL THINGS PEOPLE DO TO CELEBRATE?

ARE THERE ANY SPECIAL FOODS OR DRINKS?

IS THERE ANY STORY OR HISTORY BEHIND THE FESTIVAL?

You could even think about what you would celebrate, and how, if you created your own festival.

S.K. ALI

S. K. Ali is the bestselling author of young adult novels including *Saints and Misfits* and *Love from A to Z*. Her newest novel, *Misfit in Love*, was a *People* magazine best book of summer 2021. Her other books include the critically acclaimed anthology *Once Upon an Eid* and the bestselling picture book *The Proudest Blue*.

skalibooks.com
Instagram: @skalibooks

SHIKIRA ALLEYNE-SAMUEL

Shikira Alleyne-Samuel is a craft tutor and textile designer who holds workshops for anyone enthusiastic about sparking their inner creativity. Her work explores a variety of techniques including embroidery, print and fibre arts. She is inspired by her Caribbean heritage and the positive representation of people of colour.

kreativepursuit.com

MIKE ASPINALL

Mike Aspinall, aka The Crafty Gentleman, runs a craft blog where he teaches all sorts of craft techniques. He has presented on craft television shows and has been shortlisted for multiple craft awards. He has also written a book, *The Crafty Gentleman's Guide to Modern Paper Piecing*.

thecraftygentleman.net
Instagram: @thecraftygentleman

ALAIN BRISEÑO

Alain Briseño is a psychologist based in Mexico City. He works as a private clinical psychotherapist and teaches psychology in college. As well as being a psychologist, he is a sports fan who loves watching horror movies and feeding the hummingbirds that visit his apartment from time to time.

Instagram: @alainbriseno

QUEENIE CHAN

Queenie Chan is a manga and comic book artist whose first published work was *The Dreaming*, a mystery-horror series that has been translated into multiple languages. She has collaborated on graphic novels with authors Dean Koontz and Kylie Chan, and is currently creating *Women Who Were Kings*, a series of biographical comics about famous queens from history.

queeniechan.com
Twitter and Instagram: @queeniechanhere

JOANNE CHANG

Joanne Chang is a pastry chef and the co-owner of the Flour Bakery group and Myers + Chang restaurant. Former winner of the James Beard award, she has written five cookbooks. She teaches and advises local pastry cooks, and serves on the Board of Directors for Share our Strength. She has also appeared as a judge on the US TV baking show *Baking Impossible*.

flourbakery.com / myersandchang.com
Twitter: @jbchang
Instagram: @joannebchang

SILVINA DE VITA

Silvina de Vita is a paper artist and runs an online store called My Papercut Forest. She hand-makes and sells a range of artworks including paper-cut sculpture boxes, miniature paper domes, illustrations, prints, greeting cards and other unique objects. Forests are her favourite places in the world, and the name Silvina means 'from the woods'.

mypapercutforest.co.uk / silvinadevita.com
Instagram: @mypapercutforest

AISHANI GHOSH

Aishani Ghosh is a student at the London Contemporary Dance School. She began her training in Bharatanatyam, a form of classical Indian dance, at the age of five, and was the South Asian category finalist for the BBC Young Dancer competition in 2019. Aishani hopes to interweave her love of politics and dance in the future.

Instagram: @_aishanighosh

ERIN GLEESON

Erin Gleeson is a food writer and illustrator and author of 'The Forest Feast' cookbook series, which is all about easy vegetarian recipes filled with fruits and vegetables. She lives with her family in a cabin in the woods, where she does the watercolour illustrations for her books.

theforestfeast.com
Instagram: @theforestfeast

ISOBEL HARBISON

Dr Isobel Harbison is an Irish art critic, art historian, writer and teacher. She has curated museum exhibitions, written books and articles, and regularly gives public talks about art and culture. She loves going to galleries, libraries and archives; seeing very experimental work; speaking to artists and thinking about their art through writing.

NADIA L. HOHN

Nadia L. Hohn is an award-winning author, educator and activist who advocates for diversity in children and young adult literature. She is the author of the 'Malaika' series, and she also wrote *Harriet Tubman: Freedom Fighter* and *A Likkle Miss Lou*, among many other children's books. She is currently working on novels, picture books and plays.

nadialhohn.com
Instagram: @nadialhohn_author
Twitter: @nadialhohn

LARA LEE

Lara Lee is a chef and food writer. Her book *Coconut & Sambal: Recipes From My Indonesian Kitchen*, was named one of the best cookbooks of 2020 by several publications. She also contributes to magazines and newspapers. When she's not cooking, she's teaching Indonesian words to her young son, Jonah.

laralee.com
Instagram and Twitter: @laraleefood

TABARA N'DIAYE

Tabara N'Diaye is the founder of La Basketry, a lifestyle brand that sells kits, baskets and homeware woven with love and made in collaboration with female artisans in her native Senegal. She has written a book, *Baskets*, a stylish guide to basket-making, which is now available in six languages.

labasketry.com
Instagram: @labasketry

LESLÉA NEWMAN

Lesléa Newman has created seventy-five books for readers of all ages including the picture books, *Welcoming Elijah: A Passover Tale With A Tail; Gittel's Journey: An Ellis Island Story; Ketzel, The Cat Who Composed;* and *Heather Has Two Mummies*. She has received two National Jewish Book Awards and the Association of Jewish Libraries Sydney Taylor Body-of-Work Award.

lesleakids.com

MIQUITA OLIVER

Miquita Oliver is a television presenter and broadcaster. Formerly a co-presenter of *Popworld* with Simon Amstell, she appears regularly on British TV and radio, including on *Steph's Packed Lunch* for C4, the *Sunday Times Culture Show* and the podcast *Quiz, Chat, Repeat*. She also DJs and hosts live events.

Instagram and Twitter: @miquitaoliver

PAPA B

Papa B, aka Bodé Aboderin, is a motivational speaker and influencer who aims to shake up the fatherhood narrative. He has an IGTV series called *Papa Don't Preach* and co-hosts the weekly podcast *Pillow Talk* with his wife, the author, broadcaster and journalist Candice Brathwaite.

Instagram: @iam_papab

DOW PHUMIRUK

Dow Phumiruk is an author and illustrator of children's books, including the picture book *Hugsby*, about a little girl taking her favourite monster toy to show-and-tell. She illustrated *Counting on Katherine* by Helaine Becker and *One Girl* by Andrea Beaty. Dow is also a retired paediatrician who works part time in academic medicine.

artbydow.blogspot.com
Instagram: @dowphumiruk

MICHAEL PLATT

Michael Platt is a baker, food justice advocate and owner of a business called Michael's Desserts, a one-for-one company where for every dessert he sells, he gives one to someone in need. He also has a non-profit company called P.L.L.A.T.E (power, love, learning and access to everyone) that works around food insecurity, making sure people have equal access to food.

michaelcplatt.com
Instagram: @michaelcplatt

SAEED AL-RUBEYI

Saeed Al-Rubeyi is a fashion designer and the co-founder of a clothing brand called Story MFG. Saeed and his wife Katy design and make clothing with craftspeople using old, handcrafted methods with plant materials and natural dyes.

storymfg.com
Instagram: @saeed_storymfg

MARTA SANCHEZ

Marta Sanchez is a jazz pianist and composer who has toured the US, Europe and South and Central America performing at multiple jazz festivals. Two of her albums, *Partenika* and *El Rayo de Luz*, have appeared on the *New York Times* Top 10 Jazz Albums of the year list.

martasanchezmusic.com
Instagram: @martasanchezpiano

JULIET SARGEANT

Juliet Sargeant is a garden designer, television presenter and founder of the Sussex Garden School. In 2016 she won a Gold Medal and The People's Choice Award at the Chelsea Flower Show for her social campaigning Modern Slavery Garden. She has fellowships from The Landscape Institute and The Society of Garden Designers.

julietsargeant.com / sussexgardenschool.com
Twitter: @julietsargeant
Instagram: @julietsargeant
Facebook: @sussexgardenschool

SONALI SHAH

Sonali Shah is a television presenter and broadcaster in the UK. She is known for her roles in the BBC's coverage of many live events over recent years. These include the Queen's 90th birthday, the Royal Wedding, Wimbledon, the Commonwealth Games and the London Marathon. She has also written a children's book, *The Best Diwali Ever*.

Twitter: @SonaliShah
Instagram: @sonalishah

WENDY SHEARER

Wendy Shearer is a professional storyteller and author who performs stories in schools and cultural institutions. Her stories are drawn from her Afro-Caribbean ancestry and her degree in Classics. She has written two books: *African and Caribbean Folktales, Myths and Legends* and *Caribbean Folktales: Stories from the Islands and Windrush Generation*.

wendyshearer.co.uk
Twitter: @WCShearer
Instagram: @WendyCShearer

MARTA VELUDO

Marta Veludo is a graphic designer and art director with a studio in an old shipyard in Amsterdam Noord. Inspired by pop culture, folk art and pound shops, she designs for cultural institutions and commercial clients. She enjoys combining different disciplines and mediums to create engaging experiences.

martaveludo.com
Instagram: @martaveludo

NICK WOOD

Nick Wood is an architect, artist and founder of How About Studio, a creative practice that works at the intersection between art and architecture. He aims to imagine, design and build experiences that tell rich, engaging stories, and has worked with cultural institutions and brands in the UK and internationally.

howaboutstudio.com
Instagram: @howaboutstudio

LAURA GLADWIN

Laura Gladwin is a writer and editor specializing in food and drink, nature, crafts and art. She is the author of *Feast Your Eyes on Food: A Food Encyclopedia of More Than 1000 Delicious Things to Eat*, and lives in London with her family.

Instagram: @ljgladwin

DAWN M. CARDONA

Dawn M. Cardona is a self-taught illustrator working mainly with paper. Her dream of illustrating children's books began in 2019, but she has been cutting paper using the same pair of scissors for the past seventeen years. This is her first book in digital format.

dawnmcardona.com

THE PUBLISHER WOULD LIKE TO THANK EVERY PERSON WHO SHARED THEIR FAMILY RECIPES, STORIES AND ACTIVITIES TO MAKE THIS BOOK COMPLETE

TO MY WHOLE FAMILY, WITH LOVE AND THANKS FOR ALL THE CELEBRATIONS WE HAVE ENJOYED TOGETHER – L.G.

TO STUNKER, I COULD NOT HAVE MADE IT THROUGH THIS ONE WITHOUT YOU – D.C.

MIX
Paper from responsible sources
FSC® C104723
FSC www.fsc.org